T0328698

Cambridge Elements ≡

Elements in Historical Theory and Practice
edited by
Daniel Woolf
Queen's University, Ontario

COLLABORATIVE HISTORICAL RESEARCH IN THE AGE OF BIG DATA

Lessons from an Interdisciplinary Project

Ruth Ahnert
*Queen Mary University of London
and The Alan Turing Institute*

Emma Griffin
UEA

Mia Ridge
British Library

Giorgia Tolfo
British Library

CAMBRIDGE
UNIVERSITY PRESS

Shaftesbury Road, Cambridge CB2 8EA, United Kingdom

One Liberty Plaza, 20th Floor, New York, NY 10006, USA

477 Williamstown Road, Port Melbourne, VIC 3207, Australia

314–321, 3rd Floor, Plot 3, Splendor Forum, Jasola District Centre, New Delhi – 110025, India

103 Penang Road, #05–06/07, Visioncrest Commercial, Singapore 238467

Cambridge University Press is part of Cambridge University Press & Assessment, a department of the University of Cambridge.

We share the University's mission to contribute to society through the pursuit of education, learning and research at the highest international levels of excellence.

www.cambridge.org
Information on this title: www.cambridge.org/9781009175555

DOI: 10.1017/9781009175548

First published 2023

A catalogue record for this publication is available from the British Library.

ISBN 978-1-009-17555-5 Paperback
ISSN 2634-8616 (online)
ISSN 2634-8608 (print)

Collaborative Historical Research in the Age of Big Data

Lessons from an Interdisciplinary Project

Elements in Historical Theory and Practice

DOI: 10.1017/9781009175548
First published online: January 2023

Ruth Ahnert
Queen Mary University of London and The Alan Turing Institute

Emma Griffin
UEA

Mia Ridge
British Library

Giorgia Tolfo
British Library

Author for correspondence: Emma Griffin, e.griffin@uea.ac.uk

Abstract: *Living with Machines* is one of the largest digital humanities projects ever funded in the United Kingdom. The project brought together a large interdisciplinary team to leverage more than twenty-years' worth of digitisation projects in order to deepen our understanding of the impact of mechanisation on nineteenth-century Britain. In contrast to many previous digital humanities projects which have sought to create resources, the project was concerned to work with what was already there, which whilst straightforward in theory is complex in practice. This Element describes the efforts to do so. It outlines the challenges of establishing and managing a truly multidisciplinary digital humanities project in the complex landscape of cultural data in the United Kingdom and shares what other projects seeking to undertake digital history projects can learn from the experience. This title is also available as Open Access on Cambridge Core.

Keywords: digital history, digital humanities, British history, nineteenth century, multidisciplinarity

ISBNs: 9781009175555 (PB), 9781009175548 (OC)
ISSNs: 2634-8616 (online), 2634-8608 (print)

Contents

Authorship Statement

The text of this Element was produced collaboratively by Ruth Ahnert, Emma Griffin, Mia Ridge, and Giorgia Tolfo. It reports on the experiences of the Living with Machines Project, which was funded by UK Research and Innovation's Strategic Priorities Fund, and delivered by the Arts and Humanities Research Council. As such it rests on the experiences of the wider Living with Machines team, whose insights the lead authors collected through reflection sessions. In these sessions we invited team members to contribute written feedback and insights via structured questions and writing prompts. The authors sought to incorporate the range of perspectives and expertise in the following pages. A full list of current and past members of the team is listed below. From the team, the authors would especially like to thank David Beavan, Kaspar Beelen, Maja Maricevic, Tim Hobson, Katie McDonough, Fede Nanni, and Joshua Rhodes for their contributions.

The Living with Machines team, past and present (as of July 2022):

- Ruth Ahnert, Principal Investigator, Queen Mary University of London
- David Beavan, Co-Investigator (Co-I), The Alan Turing Institute
- Giovanni Colavizza, Co-I, The Alan Turing Institute (to June 2019)
- Adam Farquhar, Co-I, British Library (to September 2019)
- Emma Griffin, Co-I, University of East Anglia
- James Hetherington, Co-I, The Alan Turing Institute (to January 2020)
- Jon Lawrence, Co-I, University of Exeter
- Maja Maricevic, Co-I, British Library (joined September 2019)
- Barbara McGillivray, Co-I, King's College London
- Mia Ridge, Co-I, British Library
- Sir Alan Wilson, Co-I, The Alan Turing Institute
- Clare Austin, Rights Manager, British Library
- Kaspar Beelen, Digital Humanities Research Associate, The Alan Turing Institute
- Mariona Coll-Ardanuy, Computational Linguistics Research Associate, The Alan Turing Institute
- Karen Cordier, Fellowships Manager, The Alan Turing Institute (December 2021 to March 2022)
- Joel Dearden, Research Software Engineer, The Alan Turing Institute (died July 2020)
- Léllé Demertzi, Project Administrator, The Alan Turing Institute (joined June 2022)
- Rosa Filgueira, Data Architect, University of Edinburgh (to September 2019)

- Lydia France, Junior Research Data Scientist (joined July 2022)
- Sarah Gibson, Research Software Engineer, The Alan Turing Institute (May 2020 to May 2021)
- Lucy Havens, Visiting Researcher, The Alan Turing Institute (June 2022)
- Timothy Hobson, Research Software Engineer, The Alan Turing Institute
- Kasra Hosseini, Research Data Scientist, The Alan Turing Institute (to December 2021)
- Michael Jackson, Software Architect, University of Edinburgh (to July 2019)
- Amy Krause, Data Architect, University of Edinburgh (to March 2020)
- Christina Last, Research Data Scientist, The Alan Turing Institute (July 2021 to May 2022)
- Katherine McDonough, History Senior Research Associate, The Alan Turing Institute
- Federico Nanni, Research Data Scientist, The Alan Turing Institute (joined project November 2019)
- Nilo Pedrazzini, Research Associate in Corpus-Based Digital Humanities, The Alan Turing Institute (joined January 2022)
- André Piza, Research Project Manager, The Alan Turing Institute
- Griffith Rees, Research Data Scientist, The Alan Turing Institute (joined June2022)
- Josh Rhodes, Research Associate, The Alan Turing Institute (joined November 2020)
- Affiliate Yann Ryan, Curator Digital Newspapers, British Library (to January 2019)
- Guy Solomon, Research Associate, The Alan Turing Institute (joined April 2022)
- Giorgia Tolfo, Data and Content Manager, British Library
- Daniel van Strien, Digital Curator, British Library
- Olivia Vane, Digital Humanities Research Software Engineer, British Library (to November 2021)
- Kalle Westerling, Research Software Engineer, British Library (joined January 2022)
- Daniel Wilson, History Research Associate, The Alan Turing Institute

Introduction

Interdisciplinary collaboration in the humanities happens, but it is not common. The vast majority of books and articles in the humanities are single-authored. Colleagues may co-edit a volume of essays and co-write an introduction, but for most scholars in these fields that is the limit of their research collaboration. However, a number of forces have combined in recent years to make the convening of larger, and often interdisciplinary, teams a compelling and even necessary route for the study of our culture and history. The landscape of humanistic inquiry is being transformed by the increasing availability of source material at scale, created by the large-scale digitisation programmes that have been undertaken internationally by cultural heritage institutions and projects. The radical change in the scale of available material has created traction for approaches broadly characterised as 'digital humanities', which promise to make the processing of such volumes of data more feasible and to yield new analytical insights that were not possible at the level of individual documents and sources.

The opportunity promised by the computational harnessing and analysis of vast digitised collections is accompanied by a challenge, however. Traditionally scholars in the humanities have not been trained in technical or statistical skills to leverage digital content without the aid of user inter-faces. Rare are the scholars who have all of the requisite skills to undertake an end-to-end computational analysis; and, even for those with competence in these areas, the size of the task is often daunting for lone researchers. A small part of the solution to this challenge lies in the provision of additional digital training in humanities programmes. But, for the most part, interdisciplinary collaboration offers the most realistic solution: bringing together teams that combine domain specialist knowledge in the sources, and those with the technical skills to computationally leverage source material at scale.

While an increasing number of scholars are conceiving, managing and executing large-scale multidisciplinary projects in this space, the practice is still young. This means that there are few models of how to go about such a process, and those models often still remain hard to access because projects and digital humanities 'Labs' tend to focus on research outcomes rather than sharing their internal workings. While scientists in various sub-fields learn about how a lab is run from early in their research careers, by contrast historians, linguists, literature scholars, and other humanists who find themselves involved in large projects or collaborative initiatives often do not have a blueprint to look to. This means that new projects and initiatives expend a lot of energy in their start-up period trying to establish collaborative values and project management strategies, often reinventing the wheel in the process.

As humanities research moves in this direction, it is increasingly important that we think deliberately and thoughtfully about how we design, structure, and undertake collaborative research. One way of doing this is by opening the doors on the internal workings of different projects. This Element arises on a particular project called *Living with Machines* (LwM). This is a UK-based project funded by UK Research and Innovation's Strategic Priorities Fund, and overseen by the Arts and Humanities Research Council, which began in 2018 and ends in 2023. It is one of the largest investments to be made in the arts and humanities, and so it is dealing with a team much larger than normally encountered by researchers from these backgrounds. But this Element seeks to be more than a simple project report: it aspires to provide a vision of how multi- and interdisciplinary collaborative research teams can work in ways that are greater than the sum of their disciplinary parts. To do so it considers the pragmatic steps that facilitate intellectual exchange across those different disciplinary and professional contexts, which might be categorised broadly as the organisational issues of project management; legal and institutional issues of access to data; and the technical issues of hosting, wrangling, and analysing such data.

Living with Machines has a particular set of research interests: specifically to examine the ways in which technology altered the lives and culture of people in Britain during the long nineteenth century (c.1780–1920). The project is marshalling a whole range of sources that have already been digitised from maps, to census returns, to newspapers, books, and journals. The experience with working with such sources provides lessons that are relevant to scholars working with such material both within and beyond the UK context.

But this Element is primarily concerned with the broader, operational insights that the project has to yield. It was conceived from the outset as an experiment in radically interdisciplinary collaboration: it brings together data scientists, software engineers, historians, curators, library professionals, computational linguists, literary critics, and an urban geographer with the aim of undertaking research that at once offers a data-driven approach to history and a human-centred approach to data science. To achieve this we knew that we needed to build an uncompromisingly collaborative research philosophy: one that would be iterative, self-reflexive, and designed to evolve – because in collaborative work we don't get everything right the first time.

One of our key principles was that none of the represented groups or sectors should be in service of the others. Rather, we have sought to build on the skills and experiences of the whole team, not just in their domain specialisms, but in their research and management processes. From the outset we have combined ideas and frameworks from the software and project management communities with the practices and values native to the disciplines of our various collaborating team members, in the humanities, cultural heritage, social and data sciences, and brought them together in an ongoing process of exchange.

Such exchange requires openness and willingness to change. Within the team this is fostered by making a space for frequent self-reflection concerning the advantages and the limitations of the collaborative infrastructure we've set up, and aiming to remodel it whenever we identified areas of potential improvement. But progress in such areas can only really be made if scholars are committed to sharing their experiences beyond the closed systems of their projects and centres. This Element, therefore, seeks not only to share our experiences and recommendations but also to begin a conversation that invites our interlocutors to improve on our practices. As such, this Element situates itself within the rich emergent field of work on digital humanities lab culture and collaborative practice, which covers a range of forms, from informal self-published outputs such as blog posts, handbooks, charters, and white papers, to a growing number of formal published ethnographic studies and auto-ethnographies (see Sections 1 and 4).

By participating in this self-reflexive work we do not pretend to have finally solved the challenge of cross-domain collaboration. The very things that allow us to benefit from doing this kind of work are very often the things that make it so challenging: different ways of thinking, working, communicating, and sharing our outcomes. In the following pages we do, however, make a series of practical suggestions for how research projects and centres can lay foundations to make the process of exchange across these domains as productive and frictionless as possible, both at the set-up phase and in the longer-term management of a collaborative community (see especially Sections 1 and 4). These are strategies that will work as well for small teams as well as larger initiatives like our own. Indeed, on smaller projects people often underestimate how much management is required to ensure a shared vision of the desired outcomes, and how best to get there.

At the same time, however, we also identify a set of obstacles that exist within the UK research context that make data-driven humanities work more arduous and less open than it should be. One such challenge is the lack of public funding which has led to the digitisation of our national assets being undertaken by private companies that place limits on who and how people can access the digitised content. Similarly, the decision, historically, to fund projects rather than programmes has presented challenges for building and maintaining infra-structure – the time wasted building these at the outset, and the loss of resources and expertise when, all too often, infrastructure cannot be hosted and supported beyond the life of the project. These are challenges that cannot be solved by discrete projects, no matter how many strategies they have at their disposal.

For this reason, while the primary audience we imagined for this Element were individuals and teams working in the broad field of digital humanities, it is vitally important that it is also read by research funders and those shaping national policy in the digital economy and creative industries. If we are to make progress in the space of digital humanities there are challenges that need to be solved from above as well as below.

1 Starting Up

For those readers coming from humanities disciplines, or who are used to working alone, starting a new project is fairly easy. You make the decisions about what sources you will consult, negotiate access, and set timelines. You may be answerable to a funder or a line manager on your levels of productivity, but for the most part, the only person you will need to consult on intellectual decisions is yourself. A large interdisciplinary collaboration is quite a different prospect. Establishing collaborative principles, goals and ways of working requires a great deal of effort before research can even begin. The labour that this entails is almost never seen outside a project, unless those involved choose to share their practices.

This Element seeks to join the small but growing number of studies reporting on the research cultures of digital humanities projects and labs, and this section in particular is concerned with laying bare the processes undertaken in the start-up phase of such projects.[1] That body of scholarship builds on a much longer tradition of anthropological studies of scientific laboratories that began in the 1970s. In particular, a number of digital humanities scholars have looked to the scholarship of Peter Galison as a valuable model for conceptualising the processes of collaboration.[2] Galison employed the metaphor of a 'trading zone' to explain how engineers and physicists from a number of different sub-fields went about collaborating with each other to develop particle detectors and radar. The metaphor adapts anthropological studies of the development of pidgin languages and creoles in border zones to allow communication and the exchange of goods. He writes:

> Two groups can agree on rules of exchange even if they ascribe utterly different significance to the objects being exchanged . . . Nonetheless, the trading partners can hammer out a local coordination, despite vast global differences. In an even more sophisticated way, cultures in interaction frequently establish contact

---

[1] Important interventions include, amongst others, Wershler et al. (2022); and the ongoing research of Pawlicka-Deger on digital humanities working practices at https://dhinfra.org/.
[2] See, for example, Kemman (2021).

languages, systems of discourse that can vary from the most function-specific jargons, through semi-specific pidgins, to full-fledged creoles rich enough to support activities as complex as poetry and metalinguistic reflection.[3]

The metaphor provides a valuable model for thinking about how collaboration can be established. The idea of local coordination is particularly important on projects that bring together scholars from across the humanities/STEM divide but is relevant to all interdisciplinary processes. While collaboration does not require each member to understand the entire structures of the fields from which their collaborators emerge, they do need to 'hammer out a local coordination'.

The following section provides some practical strategies for enabling the members of a new project or Lab to coordinate and develop what Galison describes as 'contact languages'. This is the necessary underpinning of a stable, respectful and hybrid form of interdisciplinary collaboration. Done correctly they can create something new: Galison's 'full-fledged creoles' supporting 'activities as complex as poetry and metalinguistic reflection'. They can create new disciplinary spaces and practices in their own right. And the benefits of this are not only felt in the new field occupying that border zone. Those practices and the objects of study – the data, the methods, the historical insights, and so on – will have value too in the territories from which the collaborators have emerged. These practices and objects can be traded with those territories, perhaps encouraging others to consider travelling to the border zones in future.

By focusing specifically on the very beginning of the process of exchange we believe that this section could be particularly useful to those seeking to undertake collaborative interdisciplinary work for the first time, those who are beginning work with new collaborators or colleagues from a new field, or those seeking to scale up their collaboration to a larger team. It is not a section about how to put forward a funding bid, but rather a set of lessons about how to get a project off the ground once funding has been awarded. However, considering those steps will hopefully also help our readers think about collaboration in a way that may help them to design a better project at those earlier stages. It draws on our experience on the LwM project as a model that can yield some useful insights. While collaboration was not new to everyone on this project, some team members had never worked on interdisciplinary collaborative projects, and none of the team had ever worked on a research project of this scale, with so many people and so many separate disciplines.

---

[3] Galison (1997: 783).

While this sounds like a mythical process there are clear strategies you can employ to achieve the communication necessary to begin effectively collaborating. In the following pages we examine ways of establishing the 'rules of exchange': the importance of shared and evolving documents setting these out; their iteration in dialogue; and the establishment of spaces to build understanding and develop competency in these new contact languages.

1.1 Documenting the Rules of Exchange

When beginning a project with a new team, and recruiting into that team, it is important to have central, shared documents that express the nature of the 'local coordination' between the different disciplinary and professional fields. This is a place where the project team can express what each field gets from this exchange, and the practical steps to achieving those objectives. Max Kemman's work in digital history usefully references political scientists Gary King and Daniel Hopkins, who write: 'computer scientists may be interested in finding the needle in the haystack (such as a potential terrorist threat or the right web page to display from a search), but social scientists are more commonly interested in characterizing the haystack'.[4] Kemman argues that interdisciplinary collaborations therefore require coordination to align participants with respect to the project's goals, terminology, and desired results.[5]

The grant bid document is one step towards this coordination but is often too concise to deal with the practicalities of actually delivering that vision. This is why funding bodies often require a Delivery Plan from larger projects.

1.1.1 The Delivery Plan

This may feel like an additional administrative burden, but our experience of designing a Delivery Plan suggests that it is a valuable process for projects of all sizes. The benefits are threefold. Firstly, the conversations required to write it help a team negotiate a shared understanding of objectives and approaches, helping the team to dispense with shibboleths that may prevent clear communication. Secondly, it creates a central document that all team members can consult, and importantly update iteratively as cross-domain understanding deepens and goals evolve. Thirdly, it serves the function for which funding bodies use it – that is, to hold projects to account.

A delivery plan, therefore, should be a living document that is modified over the life of a project. The LwM plan was organised under the following headings:[6]

---

[4] King and Hopkins (2010).   [5] Kemman (2021: 42).   [6] Ahnert et al. (2019).

- Vision and objectives;
- Impact Plan – a set of goals of where your project will make a difference, ideally speaking to each of the home disciplines or professional contexts;
- Work Plan – including milestones, governance and reporting structures, and risk management;
- Finance Profile;
- Monitoring and Evaluation – including methods of monitoring, and key performance indicators (KPIs);
- Communication and Engagement Strategy.

Some of these will be particular to the individual project, and build on the team's specific expertise: the vision, objectives, impact plan, communications strategy, and financial profile will all be unique. Other headings will, however, require projects to consider many of the same things and so are worth exploring in a little more detail here.

One of these is governance – the framework and accountability that defines and controls the direction and specific outcomes from the project. Our delivery plan contains a very simple organogram (see Figure 1). While traditionally such structures are about holding projects to account, there is a more positive and collaborative way of using these structures to make use of the kind of 'agents'

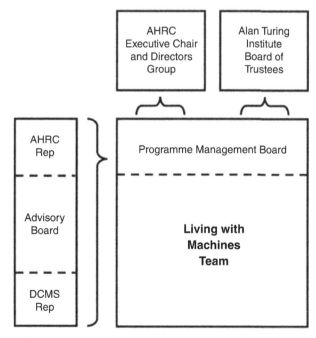

Figure 1 Organogram of the LwM project

described by Galison. Galison's study shows how trade between two or more cultures can be facilitated by agents who speak at least a little of the language of both. In our case the LwM project was designed by a team of investigators that included several people who practised in speaking across domains and were thus able to help build the vision of collaborative possibility and induct new members into that vision. They formed the project management board (PMB), which was also in charge of ensuring the rules of exchange were adhered to, developed and iterated at the right intervals as the team, its expertise, and insights evolved. It is vital that such a board meets regularly to ensure that it can respond to developments on a project, steering the intellectual vision and also ensuring that the objectives really do expand a space for new exchange whilst also enriching the home disciplines and practices (discussed further in Section 4).

Communicating effectively with overseeing structures can also be a positive experience as they can share insights from other projects to which one may not have access. The advisory board plays a particularly active role in this respect. The members of the Advisory Board were selected by the PMB, who each nominated a person from their particular domain to 'keep them honest'. We also have a member of the funding council sitting on our advisory board. This has ensured that the board has a complementary breadth of expertise to the team itself, with several people also occupying the position of agents that can facilitate exchange with the breadth of disciplines, and recommend how best to make an impact in those areas.

The interactional expertise of advisory boards, however, is often under-utilised by projects. All too often board meetings are dominated by top-line reporting on its finances, progress against milestones and KPIs, and manage-ment of risks. We believe that this is a mistake, especially in the case of highly collaborative projects, where there are often few established ways of undertaking research and delivering outputs. To tackle this missed opportun-ity, LwM made one of its two annual Advisory Board meetings a workshop at which the full team presented their research. This is a practice we would strongly recommend because of the way that it allowed the board to feed directly into the intellectual direction of the project, shaping outputs and interventions whilst still in progress, and encouraging us to position our outcomes in venues that best serve the interdisciplinary mission, as well as speaking to the contributing disciplines. Often they encouraged us that we could be more bold in our interventions. The benefits were not only for the project, however; members of the board also commented that they felt much more intellectually engaged in the venture than they were used to being in other advisory capacities.

Another mechanism that the delivery plan encourages teams to employ is the 'key performance indicator'. KPIs are designed to provide evidence for progress towards a goal. While many baulk at the way that such practices edge research further into audit culture, they have some real benefits for the team if employed wisely. The most important feature is that they require conversations around what success looks like for all the constituent members of the community, and how this can be translated into shared goals. Choosing KPIs therefore also provides an opportunity to translate your values into measurable outcomes, and ways of measuring successful progress towards those. For example, one of our key goals on LwM was 'to enable an effective collaborative environment that facilitates interdisciplinarity, and supports and promotes all members'. To measure our progress, therefore, we collected metrics on:

- The number of blog posts, conference papers, articles and other published outcomes that shared recommendations for best practice for undertaking collaborative interdisciplinary projects.
- The number of publications and other outputs that were authored by team members from two or more different disciplines, or which were placed in interdisciplinary venues;
- The number of in-team enrichment initiatives that we organised (including reading groups, workshops, peer training, etc.);
- The number of team members on fixed-term contracts to successfully transition into permanent academic/research posts or permanent industry posts.

Well-designed KPIs can therefore create precision for a broader vision, and provide the team with a set of clearly demarcated goals to which they hold themselves to account. Importantly, if they are thoughtfully designed, they can push back against the more dehumanising aspects of audit culture by making the growth, welfare, and future of the team a priority.

This set of values brings us to another piece of documentation that we would contend is vital to any project or research group, especially interdisciplinary collaborative projects: a project (or Lab) charter.

1.1.2 The Project Charter

A Delivery Plan is a useful way to article shared goals and for determining sensible steps towards those. Such documents, however, are less suited to expressing the broader culture and project ethos, and ways that a team will interact on a daily basis. To address this, one advisory board member recommended that we develop a project charter. The team of Investigators drew up a first version in advance of recruitment interviews so that it could be shared with shortlisted candidates in order that they could understand exactly what they were signing up for when they accepted a job offer. It was subsequently reworked in a full-team workshop once all members were on board to make sure that they were able to shape the terms of collaboration and bring their experience from working on other projects or in other sectors. We believe this is a practice that should become standard on all projects.

The concept of a project or Lab charter is already gaining traction in the digital humanities. Our charter is strongly influenced by the one developed by Stan Ruecker and Milena Radzikowska[7] and takes inspiration from the charter developed by Scholars' Lab at the University of Virginia.[8] It begins with a recognition that collaboration can be uncomfortable, and that it takes a proactive approach, which can be time-consuming precisely because of the way that it brings together members from different research cultures, with different expectations about how to work, and how to disseminate research findings. The charter therefore attempts to establish the foundations of Galison's 'contact language' by listing a set of informal policies or values that the team commits to abide by, but also to revisit and revise when the statements are no longer working or require nuancing. The LwM charter asserts eight values, and individual steps towards those; the six of these headings that we list here (minus their more lengthy sub-statements) have the most general application to collaborative interdisciplinary research projects:[9]

1. *We are interested in disseminating the results of this project as widely and openly as possible, with credit to us for doing so. Our policies around credit should balance both generosity and meaningfulness.*

The first of these values focuses on the dissemination of results and outcomes. It is a commitment to openness on two levels: to open and reproducible research, making available where possible our data, code, and publications in as open a format as possible; and to make visible the labour of all parties in the work we are sharing. At its core this is a value statement about authorship, but more broadly this is about crediting and valuing all the different kinds of work that go into making a project like this possible. It was, however, something quite new for members of the team from more traditional humanities backgrounds. This value is informed by The Alan Turing Institute's commitment to open research.[10] It is a topic that has required a lot of thought on the project because

---

[7] Ruecker and Radzikowska (2008).

[8] Scholars' Lab charter, https://scholarslab.lib.virginia.edu/charter/.

[9] The full charter can be found here: https://livingwithmachines.ac.uk/how-we-collaborate-3-the-project-charter/.

[10] The Turing Way Community (2019).

of the hugely different publication cultures in the team members' respective home disciplines. Understanding those different cultures and pressures takes time. This statement expresses our desire to push those norms, but not at the cost of the future employment prospects of our early career colleagues. Those particular issues are discussed in more depth in Section 4.

2. *We value meeting in person (where at all possible), and meeting regularly, in order to build community, shared understanding, and expertise.*

This second statement was grounded in the belief that sitting side-by-side is often the best way to facilitate learning, discovery, insight, and to clear blocks to progress, as well as to build a sense of community. For example, one study of the practice of pair-programming – where two programmers develop software side by side at one computer – suggests the approach not only ensures fewer bugs and mistakes in software development, but also faster progress in the development of skills, and better team morale.[11] This of course was an easier value for those team members located closer to The Alan Turing Institute, inside the British Library (BL), than it was for the four investigators located outside London; and (as for the rest of the world) it needed to be radically reimagined when the Covid-19 pandemic struck in year two of the project. However, that commitment to working together in-person in the early phase of the project ensured a sense of community that made the transition online less disruptive than it might have been had the pandemic arrived earlier in our process. In retrospect, the pandemic also made our third statement more important than it may otherwise have been:

3. *We intend this work to move forward at a steady pace, given due awareness of the vagaries of life.*

This should be a given in all professional contexts, but it helps to write it out in black and white – and we therefore recommend a similar statement should be written into all project charters. As well as the universal experience of Covid-19, we have had people depart for new jobs, retire, and, in a tragic case, pass away. We have experienced life events that have had an impact on certain individuals' ability to engage with the project for periods of time: illness, the birth of children, bereavement, and care responsibilities. If a team is to function like a community it needs to be able to flex with such events in a way that individual members feel supported and able to step back for the time necessary. That means trying where possible to organise work so that others can step in to complete a task. This relates to our fourth statement:

---

[11] Cockburn and Williams (2001).

4. *We acknowledge that this project will require an organisational effort due to its scale and ambitions, and will therefore develop and demonstrate new scholarly practices in the digital humanities.*

Frictionless collaboration is not just about intellectual exchange, but also about open ways of working, good documentation practices, and storing all documentation, code and data in repositories accessible to all those who require them (as well as ensuring their security). Such practices mean that everyone should be able to find the information they need; that when people leave the project key information does not disappear with them; and that new recruits are able to pick up the information they need as quickly and easily as possible. Such practices are becoming more common, but once again we contend they should become standard. This is discussed further in Section 4.

In our fifth and sixth statements, we laid down our guiding principles with respect to communication and teamwork:

5. *We wish to communicate in such a way as to preserve professional dignity and sanity.*
6. *We would like to foster goodwill among all the participants.*

The assumption here is that 'contact languages' are not the only thing that ensures effective collaboration. All such efforts will fail if there is not good will on a project. Once again, these may seem like a given; but having them clearly stated can be a powerful reminder in moments of stress and pressure. Under these headings, we outlined our expectations for mutual respect, assumption of good intention, and clear and transparent communication. Whilst these kinds of statements are routinely included in Project Charters, we felt that they had particular resonance for us, owing to the fact that the team was almost entirely unknown to each other at the outset. Our project did not have a deep stock of friendship and goodwill to draw upon. Therefore outlining these values and sharing them with all the team was important.

Treating the Charter as a living document projects also enables the full team to have ownership of it, which can be beneficial when challenges are faced: we can go back to, renew our commitment to its principles, and refresh wording to take into account new developments. Whilst it is unlikely to contain the answers to specific problems, it lays down the approach that we should take to conflict, and that is an enormously powerful tool. Indeed, it is difficult to imagine how the inevitable conflicts that arise with large, collaborative teams could be addressed without reference to the shared values that unite the team and we would strongly encourage any team of new collaborators to articulate their values through a document of this kind.

1.2 Creating Spaces for Exchange

You can write all the plans you like, but at some point you just need to begin working. This section explores the structures you can put in place on projects to allow people to begin the process of exchange, to develop and practice a new 'contact language', and to start work in earnest. Often this means creating smaller groups and spaces to hammer out concrete problems. These will ideally cut across the project in different ways, so different groupings can assemble around shared intellectual interests, as well as provide opportunities for full-team exchange.

The main space of exchange on a project will necessarily be structured by the research matter at hand, and its questions or topics. The grand aim of LwM was to harness digitised collections to shed new light on the impact of mechanisation on the lives of ordinary people during the nineteenth century. This however was broken down from the outset into five thematic Labs, organised around the topics of 'Language', 'Space and Time', 'Sources', 'Communities', and 'Integration, Infrastructure and Interfaces' (3I). The aim was that each Lab should have a mix of disciplinary backgrounds in their membership that would provide a multifaceted way of approaching the source materials and key historiographical issues at stake. Our next issue was how these assembled Labs should begin work. The following section is a proposal for a mechanism that we employed to good effect on LwM to deliver a first proof-of-concept piece of work for each Lab.[12] We believe it is a valuable model that could be co-opted within interdisciplinary projects or other collaborative environments for building teams and generating proof-of-concept work that could help the development of new projects and funding bids. It offers a practical strategy for facilitating exchange in a way that speeds the process towards 'full-fledged creoles'.

1.2.1 Starting Work: The Minimum Research Outcome

Taking on the large-scale questions at the heart of a research project will always be a daunting prospect for a newly assembled team. In trying to find new ways of working together, understanding each other's stake in the research problem, co-designing an approach, and deploying the best combination of skills – a team is unlikely to hit the right solution on its first attempt. To lower the stakes, one of the initial Co-Investigators (Co-Is) on the project, James Hetherington, suggested that we adapt the idea of the minimum viable product (MVP), a concept suggested by Eric Ries in 2009.[13] Conceived in the world of software development, an MVP is a product with just enough features to satisfy early customers, to test hypotheses,

---

[12] For a longer account, see Ahnert et al. (forthcoming).
[13] See Ries (2009); and Rhinow et al. (2012).

and to provide feedback for future product development. Despite its origins in software development, the concept has already been adopted by the library and heritage sectors. For example, a museum may build an MVP to test assumptions about how visitors to an exhibition will want to access further information, or a library developing a new item viewer may create an MVP to enable interim access to digitised items. MVPs encourage experimentation by time-boxing the resources required. They can limit scope creep by requiring an evaluation and consensus before either 'sunsetting' the product or moving on to the next phase of development. An MVP is flexible enough to be able to balance a long-term reflective, patient, scholarly approach with a short-term need for measurable and meaningful outputs. We adapted the MVP concept to the needs of our project's Labs, translating it into 'minimum research outcomes' (MRO).

We chose to distinguish between an *outcome* and an *output* as the objective of the MRO process because we recognised that we were unlikely to have a polished output such as a journal article, fully operational tool, or completed methods paper at the end of the process. Instead the aim was to reach a place where we had first results or proof-of-concept outcomes that could be developed in subsequent phases of the project. From design to delivery, each Lab was given nine months. The MRO process began with simple, short design documents to identify the key questions each Lab wanted to answer and what the significance of those questions was in terms of historical interest, methodological interest, and challenges for data science:

Design Document for the Minimum Research Outcome

Question of historical interest: Here, as well as the formal minimal problem statement, also specify the broader conceptual question that this relates to. Why is it interesting?

Historical methods question: Specify a *concrete* historical research question. How would solving this question help solve the question of historical interest?

Data science research question: Specify some ideas for data science approaches that might be explored in answering this question, with references.

Infrastructural approaches: What software tools, languages, and computer platforms will be used to address the question?

Why is this minimal? What other methodological questions would need to be solved besides this to make a useful historical contribution? What is the broader historical question to which this minimal question would contribute? What are you deliberately ignoring/simplifying what would need to be included if you were doing this properly? What are the minimal data sets needed to address this?

After this, what might you do next to make it less minimal?

What do you need from other labs? And how might other labs benefit from your work?

How might this be constructed as a 'function' in computer terms? NB: You do not have to actually reduce the research to this level, we just want to stimulate this kind of thinking in the labs. It shouldn't narrow your thoughts in the research programme.

Outputs plan: How do you plan to publish this work? As code, as data sets, as papers, at a conference, as articles?

References: Short bibliography.

While we recognised that each of the Labs would have different emphases, we thought it was important that each should design pieces of work that would help us move towards answering a historical question (however broadly defined), as well as making a specific methodological contribution that was not only beneficial to the history community but also could potentially generate interest and insights for data scientists – thus ensuring that no discipline or field was in the service of another. Moreover, we sought to encourage the team to think about the entire pipeline of work, from data acquisition onward, by keeping in mind what infrastructural requirements the work had.

The MRO phase concluded with a workshop at which each Lab presented its work to the rest of the team. This not only allowed all to see the work completed by the various Labs, but it also provided a process for reflecting upon the MRO as a mechanism to begin work on a large, multidisciplinary project. In most cases, the work delivered at the end of the MRO process had evolved considerably from the original design document. One example is the work undertaken by the Language Lab. The design document began with the questions: 'How have machines been represented in relation to causation and historical change? To what extent did people understand the role of machines as pre-determined and to what extent could their roles be shaped by human action?' This ultimately developed into a new method for detecting 'atypical animacy' in texts, which then paved the way for a historical study of the trope of animate machines.[14]

---

[14] Coll Ardanuy et al. (2020).

We agreed that the MRO allowed us to address a number of separate challenges and opportunities at once, but to time-box experimentation. By examining the benefits of each of the contributing fields and frameworks the design document sought to operationalise the act of translation described by Galison's trading zones metaphor. Importantly it allowed us to transition from the process of conceptualising our working methodology to actively collaborating. By keeping our scope minimal we were able, temporarily, to park the question of how our project would, in the course of time, bring together different data sets, Labs, research questions, and disciplinary perspectives into a unified whole. By allowing different sections of the project team to explore and demonstrate what they could do, we were able to evaluate the outcomes against strategic priorities and thus lay the foundations for future research directions. We believe that when a team is able to come to a broad consensus on the value of ongoing developments this helps limit mission creep and reduce the impact of 'passion projects' on shared resources. MROs that aren't taken forward may still result in publications or spin-off projects and should be documented for reference.

The review process allowed us to identify some potential improvements to the MRO concept, which we would implement in future projects and counsel others to employ. Firstly, we would advise people using this concept to keep considering how to make the outcome as minimal as possible without compromising the ultimate aims of the project. This must be supported by a willingness to iterate and to rescale expectations in response to the reality of the task. Some team members felt more pressure than others to deliver all that they had promised, which brings us to a second point, about pacing. We allowed nine months for the delivery of the MROs, and this relatively long time frame ran the risk of investing ideas that began as small experiments with an undesirable momentum. We would therefore advise users to keep in mind the sunk cost fallacy: just because time has been spent on a particular experiment does not justify continuation of that line of work if it proves not to be fruitful. One of the most durable legacies of the MROs was a switch to much shorter work iterations and to carving up tasks into smaller units (discussed further in Section 4). The point of the MRO is to learn enough about whether an idea works to decide whether to build on it, change it, or leave it behind. Such principles are much more easily stated than enacted, but a shorter cycle of work at the outset will certainly help.

1.2.2 Meeting Culture

Creating spaces for exchange, however, is not simply about big organisational structures and concepts like the MRO, but also the daily experience of co-working. As suggested above, one of the things we sought to put in place at the beginning of the LwM project was frequent co-working within the space of The Alan Turing Institute. We tried to ensure close contact by reserving a bank of ten desks for our team so they could genuinely work side by side; our team were also often to be seen co-working in the institute's communal areas. Space, however, is a luxury that many do not have; and more than ever, following the pandemic, teams are thinking creatively about how they can collaborate virtually. Whether a project has a physical base or is entirely virtual (and even largely asynchronous),[15] our experience was that some real-time meetings are necessary. We believe, therefore, that it is important to consider the meeting culture of your project at the outset as a vital ingredient to ensuring the development of the 'contact language'.

This point may seem simple and mundane, yet creating an effective meeting culture has in fact proved anything but simple. Most obviously, there are timetabling complications, particularly when attempting to schedule in-person meetings with collaborators from several different institutions, and with people who are only fractionally employed on the project. There is also a raft of more fundamental considerations, such as: What are meetings for? Who should be present at which meeting? How often should they be held? Furthermore, in a fixed-term project such as ours with a rapidly evolving pattern of work, solutions to such questions are unlikely to be stable. What might work, or be necessary, at the beginning of a project is not necessarily suitable later. With these considerations in mind, in this section we seek to describe our approaches and reflect upon what has (and has not) worked.

The most important meetings in the initial phase of the project were those held by the individual Labs. For planning and moving work forward, a rhythm of fortnightly 'sprint' meetings was put in place. The 'sprint' terminology is borrowed from Agile ways of working first outlined in the Manifesto for Agile Software Development in 2001.[16] It is a practice frequently employed both in the data science and library communities and, given the presence of both constituencies in our team, key concepts from Agile were proposed for adoption. We never worked in a fully Agile fashion (for many of the reasons that Miriam Posner has outlined in her article 'Agile and the Long Crisis of Software'),[17] but alongside the notion of the two-week work 'sprint', we also adopted the use of a 'project board', and the 'stand-up' meeting.

The fortnightly sprint meetings, held by each Lab, were used to review the Lab's progress in the past fortnight and to set the agenda of work for the next two weeks. These worked well for the team as a way of structuring both work

---

[15] See, for example, GitLab (2015).   [16] See *Manifesto for Agile Software Development*.
[17] See Posner (2022).

and meetings, allowing the Lab members to break down their research agenda into small manageable tasks, and provide visibility of who was doing what. Plans for the fortnight and progress were recorded on the Lab's project board. Such boards can be a physical whiteboard or a piece of software such as the kanban board feature in Trello; we employed GitHub as this is also the place where the project keeps all its code and documentation. In its simplest version a project board will have three columns: the backlog of tasks to be done, the 'in progress' column, into which you move tasks to be undertaken in the forthcoming sprint, and the 'done' column into which tasks are moved once completed. Ideally all the 'in progress' tasks should move over at the end of the fortnight, although we were not always very good at this in the early days as we had yet to learn what two-week-sized tasks looked like. Some teams will add a 'review' column if a task needs additional eyes on it before it can be ticked off. This structure has been a very effective way of working and we would recommend it unreservedly for any collaborative team because of how it brings together a team to make collaborative decisions and allows them to document those in the process.

Given the success of the sprint meetings, we expected another idea from Agile might work just as well – the 'standup' meeting. In many organisations a standup is a daily meeting (in our case weekly), literally conducted standing up in order to encourage brevity. The idea is that each member takes two minutes to say what they are working on, and where they are experiencing blocks, with the idea that sharing these could quickly help resolve such issues. However, these meetings were never very well attended. Despite being a meeting designed to enhance collaboration, Posner has suggested that they can be perceived as a emblematic of more top-down structures:

> standups, billed as lightweight, low key check-ins, have become, for some workers, exercises in surveillance. Particularly when work is decomposed into small parts, workers feel an obligation to enumerate every task they've accomplished. There's also pressure for every worker to justify their worth; they are, after all, employees, who need to be perceived as earning their salaries.[18]

Interestingly, we found that more people responded when this activity stopped being a meeting and was transferred to an online messaging app (Slack) during the move to remote working at the beginning of the pandemic. At the same time we reframed the prompts to be open questions: (1) What is something you'd like the team to know? (2) What is something that you'd like help on? The need for social connection was likely a factor, but whatever the

---

[18] Posner (2022).

reasons, we found that many more members of the team showed up and responded to one another's answers. Therefore, we would recommend that if you are trying to do something lightweight like a standup to ensure that it really is as lightweight as possible, and framed to make people feel like a team.

Beyond the Agile concepts that we employed, we built in a regular 'thinking' meeting, that sat above and across all of the separate labs and to which all team members were invited. It initially operated as a history reading group (later known as the 'Hypothesis Generation' meeting), whereby investigators and researchers from all the various different disciplinary backgrounds met to discuss key articles and scholarly books on the transition towards living with machines in nineteenth-century Britain. The reading group served a dual function: it was used by those with humanities backgrounds to brush up on their understanding of key debates, and also for introducing team members from very different intellectual backgrounds to the specific concerns and opportunities for intervention in the historiography. As the project has evolved, so too has the name, form and function of this fortnightly thinking meeting, yet it still remains a place where intellectual or conceptual issues that straddle different branches of the project can be considered, and we warmly recommend it to any multidisciplinary project or large project with several constituent parts.

One final way that we sought to create space for exchange was through peer training. Some things all team members needed to know. We needed everyone to know how to be able to use the project management tools within GitHub (where we have our project boards alongside our code), so we provided training on this at the outset. In other cases individual team members or subsets of the team decided they wanted to improve certain skills and so would self-organise a series of sessions working through a pertinent textbook. We also organised weekly sessions called Coffee and Code, at which members of the team struggling with a technical issue could get help from one of the research software engineers or data scientists. This kind of peer training is a wonderful way for contact languages to develop on a project, and for team members to gain greater fluency in the languages of other disciplines. However, while it is something that we would recommend in the start-up phase of the project, this kind of enrichment is hard to sustain as the urgency to produce research outputs increases – and this is probably a good thing. A team needs to find its equilibrium: enough of the 'semi-specific pidgins', as Galison has it, ensure the collaborators can communicate clearly, without the pressure to become fluent in more than one field.

This equilibrium is true of meeting culture too. Our project found that, at the outset, team members wanted to attend the meetings of almost all the Lab sprint meetings, as well as the other enriching meetings mentioned above, as a way of staying abreast of new developments. Although meetings worked as a way of sharing regular updates about all the different threads of work and were certainly preferable to discussion over email, there was soon a sense that precious time was wasted simply catching up. In effect, we quickly hit up against the difficulties of running a truly multidisciplinary project and of radical collaboration. Our goal was to converge work strands and develop narratives that drew together into research arcs that traverse the breadth of our approaches and findings. But an overly busy meetings calendar did not serve those aims; it simply ate into the time available for actual research. We would suggest therefore that while an inclusive approach is probably beneficial in the start-up phase of a project, as you move beyond those first months it is vital to modify the length, frequency, and membership of meetings in order to make them more effective and productive. Our experience suggests that this will likely be an ongoing process, and we therefore explore longer-term strategies in Section 4.

1.3 Conclusions

The start-up phase of a project is a vital one, especially in highly interdisciplinary collaborative projects: it is a period in which project leaders should focus on creating the governance, reporting, community values, and pragmatic structures that will guide and shape the project throughout its life. There is a considerable journey between the award of a funding grant and the operation of a fully functioning team; and the larger grant, the more complex this journey is to navigate. The key challenge is establishing a research agenda whilst the people and ideas needed to shape and drive that agenda are still in the process of assembly. Galison's concept of trading zones is a useful one for helping teams to determine a pragmatic approach to determining first the rules of exchange, and then investing in the spaces that will allow team members to fully develop contact languages.

In all these ventures we would counsel teams to recognise what is enough. Collaboration is by definition a pragmatic process: people are partnering to do work together because they do not have all the disciplinary skills to undertake the work themselves, or the task is too large. Is the pidgin language enough to communicate? Then you probably do not need to gain a whole new raft of skills at this time. Do you know everything you need to know to do your work? Then you are probably attending enough meetings. The MRO concept that we propose above is also a pragmatic structure: it is designed to be enough work to act as a proof of concept, and allow the researchers to decide whether it is worth pursuing in its fully fledged form.

Creating a collaborative environment, however, is just one dimension of the challenges experienced in the start-up phase of a project. On digital humanities projects such as ours there are two further dimensions to consider: accessing and processing the data; and establishing the infrastructures needed to store and analyse that data. These are the topics of our next two sections.

2 Using Digitised Historical Collections

Digital projects need data with which to work. Many books and articles talk about the exciting possibilities unleashed by large digital collections, but relatively few talk about the practical steps in getting hold of such data, and the restrictions with which it may come. This section sets out the challenges in the UK-specific context of copyright legislation and digitisation funding that creates a 'mixed-rights' landscape of cultural heritage data, and the problems this poses for projects like ours in terms of accessing the data and handling it in ways that adhere to legal precedents and specific contractual agreements. More broadly we consider how the patchwork approach to digitisation both nationally and internationally has created digital collections that are far from representative.

We suggest that individual projects can make some pragmatic decisions working with the current reality, which include building collaborative relationships with cultural heritage institutions holding the data with which you are concerned; employing a rights assurance manager where funding allows; and phasing work so that data can be secured during start-up phase (although long lead-times can make this challenging within the standard funding frameworks). Future research in this space also needs to focus more on the foundational work required to determine the shape and biases of the digital collections made through piecemeal policies, and what we can do with that information – both in terms of future digitisation decisions, and in the kinds of questions we can ask of such data sets. More broadly, however, this section calls for a recognition that the challenges with which the research community are presented cannot be solved by project-level interventions. Key changes are required at the level of funding council priorities and national policy, with regard both to national infrastructure and copyright law.

2.1 The UK Context

The UK government's Department for Digital, Culture, Media & Sport (DCMS) expressed ambitions for using machine learning and data tools with digitised collections in their 2016 Culture White Paper.[19] Our project, LwM, can be seen as a test of how easy it truly is to seize such opportunities. Its objective was not

---

[19] Department for Digital, Culture, Media & Sport (March 2016).

the creation of new digital resources, but rather the leveraging of existing digitised content, to show what is possible *now*. Our focus has been on the steps that make that possible: accessing that data and making it usable for computational analysis, the generation of suitable infrastructure components and methods, and using this to generate new insights about the coming of the machine age and its impact on the lives of ordinary people.

This section deals with the first of those steps: accessing the UK's existing digital resources for the purpose of academic research. One might imagine that working with already-digitised content saves researchers time and work, enabling them to start with research on day one of the project. But the reality is a lot more complex due to the messy and variegated landscape of cultural data in the United Kingdom. While the details of our situation are particular to the United Kingdom, there are general lessons for other national contexts where researchers are working between open and privately digitised content.

Working with cultural heritage data at scale requires a keen understanding of the institutional politics of the organisations and projects that created it, and the larger national policy and funding context that has in turn shaped those policies. The body of digitised resources at our disposal is the result of a mixed economy of funding. Whilst a few small-scale digitisation projects have been funded by public money so their data is freely available'?, data from of the biggest initiatives are not available on an open access basis. UK cultural policy encourages cultural heritage institutions to create new income streams based on digital assets in order to ensure diversification and sustainability of income (see for example the recommendations of the 2017 Mendoza Review),[20] and recommends that they create digital products that appeal to a diverse section of the general public. Institutions are thus placed in the position of seeking to balance their commitment to provide access to their resources, whilst not closing their doors to commercial investments.

There are different models for such commercial partnerships. Providers like Gale and Proquest tend to specialise in the academic market; whilst they are open to working with academics, they also tend to create closed infrastructures which are not best suited for open digital research in the long term. Additionally, there are commercial providers such as FindMyPast and Ancestry catering to the large and lucrative genealogy market. These too are generally willing to share data with academic partners but have little interest in investing time and resources in creating and supporting infrastructures that will support long-term academic work. Yet despite the fact that these kinds of commercial partnerships are not designed with the interests of

---

[20] Mendoza (2017).

academic research in mind, for financial reasons they are the only route for most large cultural organisations to digitisation of their collections.

These developments are, in many ways, diametrically opposed by the impetus within the research community towards open and reproducible research. This impetus is coming at once from above and below. Initiatives like *The Turing Way* community-authored handbook are calling for the sharing of data and code underpinning research outcomes to become a standard practice, and providing practical guidelines for how to do this.[21] UK Research and Innovation (UKRI), the non-departmental public body of the government that oversees the individual research funding councils, has recently introduced an open-access policy to ensure that findings from research funded by the public through UKRI can be freely accessed, used and built on. The policy currently applies to journal articles and from 1 January 2024 will apply to monographs, book chapters, and edited collections as well. While we as a team are strongly aligned with the values of open access, it is worth pointing out the irony of one branch of government policy pushing digital collections behind paywalls, while another mandates the open access of academic research using such collections.

The question of how to work in reproducible ways with data to which access is restricted is an ongoing problem for those working in the digital humanities. For obvious reasons, commercial partners are unwilling to sign up to the free and open sharing of data and results, so a considerable amount of foundational work is required before projects can get to play with data. By sharing our experiences around key data sets we hope to make clear how this work can be handled efficiently, and where there may be larger obstacles that need to be tackled at the level of national policy.

2.2 Accessing Data

Working with cultural heritage data in the United Kingdom under the current conditions requires researchers to make a series of pragmatic decisions. Traditional history projects usually depend on finding the *best* archival collections to answer the question at hand; the only barrier might be travelling to them or gaining access to the relevant collection. When processing data at scale, one needs to consider the important trade-offs between ease of access, the benefits (and costs) of scale, and fit with your research questions.

In this section we describe the process of gaining access to several important data sets for the study of nineteenth-century life:

---

21 The Turing Way Community (2019).

- the BL's digitised newspapers, and specifically their British Newspaper Archive, digitised by FindMyPast;
- Nineteenth-century census returns, digitised by FindMyPast and processed by an ESRC-funded project to produce a data set known as the Integrated Census Microdata;
- Ordnance Survey maps, digitised and georeferenced by the National Library of Scotland;
- A collection of digitised eighteenth- and nineteenth-century books held at the BL and digitised by Microsoft.

The case studies are included here for two purposes. Firstly, they are significant data sets with which many researchers may wish to work, and some readers may thus benefit from understanding the specific steps in accessing them. Secondly, they elucidate the larger structural issues besetting researchers wishing to work with cultural heritage collections at scale.

The Investigators were aware that reliance on pre-digitised collections would throw up complex rights issues, and we therefore factored this into the initial bid through the inclusion of two roles – a Rights Assurance Manager and a Data and Content Manager. Notwithstanding the presence of appropriate expertise within the project, the complexity of the cultural data landscape made access a more arduous and time-consuming task than we initially anticipated, and a key issue that future projects tackling these and similar corpora should bear in mind within their projected timeframes.

2.2.1 Newspapers

The BL has a very large newspaper collection, comprising more than 600,000 bound volumes of newspapers (occupying 32 kilometres, or 20 miles, of shelving) and over 300,000 reels of microfilm (occupying a further 13 kilometres, or 8 miles, of shelving). The digitisation of this collection has been ongoing for a number of years. A first tranche of digitisation began in the early 2000s, through the JISC Digitisation Programme, funded by a £10 million investment by the Higher Education Funding Council for England. However, the resulting JISC data set is small and, because the digitisation was undertaken some years ago, much 'dirtier' than more recent digital data.[22] Our goal was to work with the much larger and more recently digitised collection, of which the JISC data is just a part, known as the British Newspaper Archive (BNA).

---

[22] A cleaned version was produced and redeposited by the LwM team as part of Beelen et al. (2022).

The BNA is a partnership between the BL and FindMyPast to digitise the BL's vast holdings. To date they have digitised over 60 million pages, which amounts to over 9 per cent of the BL's holdings and, increasing daily. As such it contains a vast quantity of data that speaks to the events in people's lives, from news items and reports to family notices, letters from local communities, and advertisements of the products that people would have had in their homes.

It is necessary to draw a distinction between the Library's rights and ownership of the newspapers on the one hand, and of the digital versions of their collection on the other. So long as the material is already out of copyright, the BL can make the data it owns openly available. However, out-of-copyright items in the BL's collection may still be subject to contractual restrictions if the collection has been digitised by another party. That was the case for the BNA data with which we hoped to work, which had been digitised by FindMyPast. We therefore needed to obtain the data set from this commercial partner, along with the permission to use it.

In contrast to previous newspaper projects, which have used the BNA data set by running code on FindMyPast's servers,[23] we negotiated a full data transfer. In fact, we believe that LwM is the first project to acquire such a large data set consisting of UK newspapers from an individual company. However, while FindMyPast were happy to share the data, the cogs turned slowly in acquiring data beyond a first sample (provided at the very outset), due to the need to draw up a bespoke agreement determining the terms of the data transfer.

The data transfer direct from FindMyPast was also important for another reason: so that we could lawfully analyse material that may still be in copyright. Currently in the United Kingdom, copyright expires seventy years after the author's death, or seventy years after the end of the year of the item's publication if the author is unknown. While all our newspapers are from pre-1920, at the outset of the project the BL had a 'safe date' policy that viewed any newspaper and other collections that were less than 140 years old and too large for manual clearance as potentially containing in-copyright material. This policy was necessary because a young writer could have published something in a newspaper in 1900 aged 20, and lived until they were 100, meaning only a couple of decades had passed since their death – although this scenario remains very unlikely as bylines were not common in the period. Copyright clearance generally gets more complex for more recent collections, making work with late nineteenth- and twentieth-century collections more challenging. One way to circumvent this is via a stipulation in the Copyright, Designs and Patents Act of 1988 which states that a person who has lawful access to the work

---

[23] See, for example, Lansdall-Welfare et al. (2017) and Dzogang et al. (2016).

can carry out text and data mining. This legal access clause, however, does not allow deposit libraries to supply additional copies of in-copyright material for data analysis, and so it was vital that we dealt directly with FindMyPast.

Once in receipt of the data from FindMyPast, we were permitted to analyse it and to share derived data sets, including, for example, samples of newspaper articles, to release alongside our research publications in order to make research reproducible. But due to its commercial value we cannot share larger portions of the data set, and we must keep the data in a suitably secure environment (on which, see Section 3). Moreover, while the data can be kept in storage for two years beyond the project end date (to check results for articles and other outputs in progress), beyond that date it must be deleted. We might add here that on top of the process of negotiation, one must also factor in the time it takes to transfer 58TB of data (during a pandemic, through cloud transfer), and the need to preprocess the data before analysis could begin.

While resolving these issues was an important step for our project, it is important to consider what it means for the potential of future collaborations between other cultural heritage organisations and academic institutions. The key challenge was the transfer of data between spaces, from the data owner (BL) to the owner of the infrastructure (The Alan Turing Institute). While there have been many previous examples of out-of-copyright and non-commercial content shared from the BL to other institutions, this project was the first time that they were able to put the process to the test with some challenging data and content. In particular, our work shines a light on how the text and data mining copyright exception remains untested and difficult to use in many innovative scenarios requiring the use of diverse data sets. Its goal is to enable new types of research using content published in the United Kingdom without endangering the commercial rights of content creators and owners. However, our experience shows that its application is not straightforward in enabling the innovative work at the intersection of technology and culture that is being called for as a national priority. At the time of writing, and following an extensive public consultation, the UK government is planning to introduce a new copyright and database exception which allows text and data mining (TDM) for any purpose.[24]

2.2.2 Census Data

The second example that we want to identify is an important UK data set known as the Integrated Census Microdata (or I-CeM), a vital source for capturing the impact of mechanisation on everyday lives. This data set presents some of the same challenges as the newspapers, due to the process of its

---
[24] Intellectual Property Office (2022).

production. The original census enumerators' returns are held by The National Archives, and were, like the newspapers, digitised by FindMyPast. However, and in contrast to the BL's newspaper collection, the digitised census returns have also been cleaned and coded by public funds: the Economic and Social Research Council-funded I-CeM project.[25] This public investment carried the requirement that the resulting data set be deposited with the UK Data Service (UKDS), which should, in theory, have made academic researchers' access to the data far more straightforward.

This has not, however, been our experience. Despite the expectation that publicly funded projects deposit their data sets with UKDS, a clause allows digital data owners to 'safe-guard' their data, a practice that applies either to protect personal interests (though this is rarely invoked) or commercial interests.[26] The census data forms the central plank of FindMyPast's subscription service to (mainly) family historians, so these access restrictions have been invoked to protect the commercial interests of FindMyPast, who provided the underlying transcriptions used in the original I-CeM project.

In place of unrestricted access to the full I-CeM data set via UKDS, researchers have two options. FindMyPast has deposited a simplified version with UKDS, I-CeM: SN 7481 Integrated Census Microdata (I-CeM), 1851–1911. This version includes all data about individuals recorded by the census except, crucially, their names and street addresses. As this data is anonymised, the UKDS does not stipulate any special conditions on access or storage beyond agreement to their standard End User Licence. This has the advantage of being straightforwardly and immediately accessible to anyone with a UKDS account. However, as an anonymised version of the census, it excludes four data columns containing names and addresses, as well as a number of enriched fields developed as part of the I-CeM project. Of course, many academic projects, including our own, require access to these missing columns. As an alternative, therefore, researchers can seek to access the safeguarded version – SN 7856 Integrated Census Microdata (I-CeM) Names and Addresses, 1851–1911: Special Licence Access – through the application of a special licence.

This is the process which we used to acquire the data, but it is worth noting that this mechanism effectively excludes the public. As Richard Rodger has pointed out 'just when for the first time historians, and the general public, have the capacity to manage large data sets themselves through Open Source software and, for spatial analysis, through OpenStreetMap, that opportunity is denied to them because of

---

[25] The Integrated Census Microdata (I-CeM) Project, ESRC Ref: RES-062–23-1629, was a collaboration between the University of Essex, the University of Leicester, and with a commercial partner 'FindMyPast'. Schurer et al. (2020).

[26] Rodger (2020: 135).

restricted access to the key Census elements – names and addresses'.[27] The exclusion of the public is an issue in and of itself – there is clearly an ethical concern that users must pay a fee to access resources already funded from tax-payers' money.

Furthermore, even for academic users such as ourselves with the option to apply for a special licence to access the full data set, that process proved difficult and drawn out. The process was complicated by the fact that there is often a considerable time lag between the completion of funded projects and the deposit of the data at UKDS. As a result, we needed to conduct a number of discussions with the holders of recently cleaned census data in tandem with FindMyPast in order to ensure we not only cleared the rights to the data but also obtained the best versions of the data available.

Secondly, a warning for those facing an application for a Special Licence: the forms require a not insubstantial amount of work; they are required for every team member and must be underwritten by the host organisation, a process that is more complicated when there are more than twenty staff employed by six different organisations. These then take some months for UKDS to process. Additional work to acquire agreements from UKDS and the data holders was required to allow for changes to how we would store and access the data following the move to home working during the first wave of the Covid-19 pandemic, due to the data service's outdated idea that remote access to Cloud storage could not be made secure. Moreover, while it is understandable that the licence prevents us from sharing the original data, this is not the only restriction. The data depositor is permitted to scrutinise all outputs before publication, 'at least 30 working days before the proposed publication date to enable the data depositor to consider it and comment as regards compliance with the licence conditions and for changes to be made to the publication in light of these comments'.

These hurdles place some significant barriers in the way of studying the nineteenth and early twentieth centuries through a digital humanities lens. In both the cases of the newspapers and I-CeM, there was the initial difficulty of obtaining the digital data in a timely fashion. In response to these rights difficulties, we might have scaled back our ambitions to work only on data sets that were already available on permissive terms. But we felt that required too great a degree of compromise, forcing us to adapt our project to the most easily available data, rather than our research agenda determining the data set. Instead, we pursued the data sets of our choice, accepting that there would be complex negotiations requiring lots of legal time, and appointing project

---

members to oversee this work. We would underscore, however, the need to build in time into project start dates and work plans for the execution of this vital work. The difficulty here is that the current time-frames of this process are not compatible with publicly funded projects, which are by necessity time-limited in nature and assume a quick start from day one. There is also the more intractable problem of producing reproducible research. With respect to both the BL's library corpus and TNA's census holdings, we have found that the conditions surrounding their digitisation do not lend themselves easily to reproducible research.

2.2.3 More Permissive Data Sets

Thankfully not all our data sets were as challenging to acquire. It is important to recognise that some institutions have useful data sets that are made available under permissive terms, and where this is the case, research can be more swiftly be moved forwards. We worked with a number of additional collections, and wish to highlight two key ones here.

The first is the Ordnance Survey maps. Maps provide a visual record of the changing impact of industrialisation on the landscape and are being scanned by the thousands at cultural heritage institutions around the world. In the United Kingdom, major collections like the BL, National Library of Scotland (NLS), National Library of Wales, and others have been leaders in establishing ways to make maps discoverable and re-usable for research and public engagement applications. Our own project has drawn heavily on the work of the NLS. Since 2014, the NLS has been able to scan over 20,000 sheet maps per annum, and now has over 250,000 maps available online. Although the NLS needed to partner with external organisations to fund part of the map scanning work, they have made those images freely viewable online,[28] and the associated geo-data available for non-commercial use according to the principles of open and reproducible research.[29] As a result, there are numerous examples of projects using the NLS's maps data.[30]

Secondly, a hugely valuable data set – made use of by the Language Lab – was a collection of approximately 68,000 books made freely available by the BL: 'Digitised printed books (18th–19th century)', also known informally as 'Microsoft Books'. This collection was the result of an abortive digitisation initiative by Microsoft in 2011 who gave up on the project at an early stage and

---

[28] However, programmatic access to most of the scanned collections is not open and requires negotiation with NLS. There are also some restrictions on the re-use of these maps, see: https://maps.nls.uk/copyright.html.

[29] See https://maps.nls.uk/guides/georeferencing/.   [30] See https://maps.nls.uk/projects/.

gave permission to the BL to use the underlying text and images in any way the Library wished. As public domain items, they are available for any form of re-use, unlike subsequent projects such as Google Books which remain unavailable en masse to researchers: the data set can simply be downloaded from the BL's website.[31] It should be noted, however, that Microsoft did not take a systematic approach to the selection of volumes to scan, which has resulted in a collection which if not random is at least arbitrary in its contents, and includes a mix of novels but also geography, history and other non-fiction genres. This heterogeneity means that users need to think carefully about whether it meets the needs of their research. Members of our team with BL staff have sought to make the data set more useful by developing a model to predict whether a book in this collection is fiction or non-fiction based on the title of the book.[32]

The ease with which Microsoft Books is available to the public recommends it as a prime candidate for digital research. The lack of friction even invites researchers to design questions around it. This should be the benchmark against which other data sets are measured. While the BL's Microsoft Books was a happy accident, it is part of a wider effort of the BL Labs to support and inspire the use of the Library's digital collections. The NLS is also leading the way in this area. While full programmatic access to the OS maps requires negotiation with NLS due to the terms of the creation of this resource, they have sought to make numerous other data sets easily available through their 'Data Foundry'.[33] Although we haven't made use of it in our project, it is a wonderful model of how cultural heritage organisations can lower the bar to people using their collections data. Ultimately, while it is great to see national libraries leading the way, if the government is calling for competitive research at the interface of AI and culture, it should not be left to individual institutions to shoulder the burden alone. A more consistent national approach needs to be adopted, and the infra-structure provided to support this, as we suggest at the end of this section.

2.3 Interrogating our Data for Biases

Undeniably, working with digitised collections was challenging. The simple fact of acquiring both the data and the rights to use it was complex and called for more time and resources than we had anticipated at the outset. But there was one other piece of work we needed to conduct before getting to work on our primary research questions, and that concerned the nature and coverage of the digitised data sets that we were working so hard to access.

---

[31] See www.bl.uk/collection-guides/digitised-printed-books.
[32] See https://huggingface.co/BritishLibraryLabs/bl-books-genre.   [33] See https://data.nls.uk/.

The humanities scholars on LwM came to the project with an interest in investigating the theoretical problems posed by working with large data sets. Such scholars typically work with relatively small collections and are thus regularly forced to confront the question of how representative their evidence is of the wider historical issues they wish to discuss. As humanities scholars are well aware, archives do not capture the historical world as it once existed. They are social creations. An initial process of selection determines which records and documents were produced. A second process then determines which historic records are curated and preserved in archives and libraries for later generations. In the case of digitised collection, yet another process is overlain upon these two, as archives, libraries and commercial companies make decisions about which parts of their collection merit digitisation, whether on commercial, conservation, or other grounds. In order to grapple with the question of whether our digital data sets were representative, we needed to develop a strong understanding of the structure of digitised corpora and to identify biases and absences.

These problems of overlapping biases were particularly acute for the newspaper archives. In contrast to the census and OS maps, where the digital collections largely reflect the records as originally produced, we knew that the BL's newspaper collection, vast as it is, is nonetheless an incomplete set of all newspapers published, particularly in the early decades of the newspaper industry. And their digitised newspaper collections are a still smaller set of their incomplete hard copy collection. Furthermore, successive newspaper digitisation priorities were established in collaboration with a commercial company established to serve the genealogy market, and as such may have missed periods or regions that are important from a scholarly perspective. As our rights manager worked with FindMyPast to gain access to this immense data set, and (as we will discuss in further detail in the next section) our data scientists worked on building a secure infrastructure for storing it, we nonetheless understood that what we were poised to receive constituted but a small sample of the total number of newspapers published during the nineteenth century. We therefore wanted to know more about the extent to which the digitised subset that we had represented the wider universe of nineteenth-century press titles.

Our task here was made easier by the existence of the Newspaper Press Directories (NPD), a set of volumes that were published almost annually by Charles Mitchell from 1846 onwards. These volumes were initially intended to keep a more 'dignified and permanent' record of the press.[34] In the event, the

---

[34] Gliserman (1969).

directories emerged as an authoritative list of London and provincial news-papers. Each volume provided an alphabetical list of newspapers published within that year, providing information about details considered to be of interest to proprietors and advertisers, including titles, coverage, circulation, and polit-ical persuasion, with special attention given to the interests and orientations of the producers and their audiences. Mitchell's catalogue gave proprietors space to profile their publication and helped advertisers (who wanted to buy space in those newspapers) find the right audience. The NPDs also helped us to navigate difficulties such as the frequent name changes of some titles. For example, *The Athletic Reporter* in 1886 became *The Reporter*, which in 1888 became *The Midland Counties Reporter and General Advertiser*, which in 1889 became *The Reporter and General Advertiser*, and so on.

The digital newspaper collection is very large, but size in itself is no guaran-tee against bias, such as the over-representation of newspapers claiming to be 'conservative' or 'liberal', or the under-representation of certain regions. The directories allowed us to contextualise the digital newspaper collection and better understand the corpora. We made an early decision to digitise (and transcribe with OCR software) Mitchell's the complete run of NPDs to aid us in our task of contextualisation. By extracting information from the directories and building individual profiles for each newspaper, we were able to make explicit the diversity of voices embedded in the collection and to account for gaps and biases in the composition. We called this method of analysing a digital sample in relation to the wider landscape of nineteenth-century newspapers the 'environmental scan'.

Understanding the relationship of our collection of digital newspapers to the actual collection of printed newspapers that had once circulated in Victorian Britain permitted us to explore the biases that develop through the processes of collecting and digitising, and allows for a critical inspection of the corpora and results derived from them.[35] As the team members behind the environmental scan explain, 'the point of the Environmental Scan is not to eliminate bias, but rather to provide scholars with tools that can help them understand and work with it. By better understanding the characteristics of a collection they will be better able to develop findings and interpretations sensitive to historical context'.[36]

We believe that all digital humanities projects should write steps into their work plans to think about how to interrogate the contours of their data. In the case of newspapers, our method could readily be adapted to other national contexts, many of which had similar press directories. Similarly other kinds

---

[35] Beelen et al. (2022).   [36] Beelen et al. (2022: 18).

of text or collection items may be evaluated if the correct contextual source can be found. There is clear value in collaborating with cultural heritage organisations, with a deep understanding of their holdings as well as knowledge of catalogues and other reference works that could serve such a purpose. Furthermore, work of this nature has the capacity to feed back to the holders of collections. We know that some voices are systematically excluded or marginalised in the archives and that the costs of digitisation ensure that digitisation projects will never be complete. In order to produce more systematic and representative digitised collections in the future, we need to begin with initiatives like this.

We would contend, however, the potential of the work of the environmental scan goes beyond cultural heritage data. It represents a commitment to the critical investigation of our sources and their biases that should underpin any large-scale computational analysis. As more tasks in our world are undertaken by large language models – which are now capable of producing text automatically in ways that have already begun to replace human writers of formulaic journalism – we need to make sure that the underlying data is subjected to this kind of scrutiny, so that the model does not reproduce the biases of its training data.[37] The language model recently shared by Meta (Facebook), and trained on material including a Reddit data set, is a case in point: the company's own documentation states that it has 'a high propensity to generate toxic language and reinforce harmful stereotypes'.[38]

2.4 Conclusions

As humanities scholars begin increasingly to trade in data, they need to acquire new skills. Not only does it entail scaling up skills in source criticism to collections of an entirely different order of magnitude, but it also enters a new terrain of data acquisition and access negotiations.

While the experience of our project is in many ways highly specific, because of its particular research questions and target collections, our experience of accessing previously digitised material and data sets will be typical of many projects. Working with previously digitised data should, theoretically, be easier than creating new resources. This is a reasonable expectation: we are at a phase in the evolution of digital humanities work when the previous investment into creating digital resources and data sets should be paying off for the wider community. The reality, however, is that a large proportion of our data sets – even those produced from the national collections held by publicly funded

---

[37] Bender et al. (2021).   [38] Zhang et al.(2022).

bodies – currently sit behind paywalls because those institutions were compelled to make commercial deals to fund the digitisation process.

There are ways around these paywalls. Working directly with cultural heritage institutions can be an option. This will often require accessing the data on site to ensure legal access for text and data mining, but complexity is added if the work requires large compute resources (discussed further in Section 3). This was a problem that was particularly galling for our project: despite their co-location in the same building, The Alan Turing Institute and the British Library are separate institutions, and therefore Turing offices are not included in 'on premises' access. The other option requires academics, who have little to no commercial training, to work with private companies, who have scant experience with academic projects. The negotiations are more complex than can be undertaken by academics, and therefore if budgets allow we would strongly recommend the employment of a dedicated rights manager. Although this can be costed into the project, a rights manager is only able to start work once funding has been secured. Work can of course be phased, but the current timeframes that data acquisition processes can entail make it incompatible with publicly funded projects, which are by necessity time-limited in nature.

Clearly, the issues here go beyond anything that can be addressed by individual projects: these are structural problems that need policy-level solutions. We should begin with the dream: public investment in digitisation to create *genuinely* open data sets for research and public use. Indeed, many academics would argue that it should not be a dream when other nations have achieved it for collections of national importance, including genres discussed in Section 2.2, such as newspapers and census returns. But arguing that this is a priority for national spending is a challenging case to make, especially in the current moment of economic crisis. Moreover, in the United Kingdom it would require an about-face from the government's current cultural policy, which encourages cultural heritage institutions to create their own income streams.

The problems of accessing data in the current mixed-rights landscape could be radically simplified, however, with the right publicly funded infrastructure. We might imagine a system that acts as a kind of 'digital reading room' or 'cultural heritage sandbox', as it has been described on LwM, in which data sets could be deposited by data owners and accessed virtually by users without having to jump through the numerous acquisition hoops. It could be designed not only to deal with simple open data but also data with complex rights issues, so that users could access it via a kind of black box process: in the case of commercially owned or sensitive data that users were not actually permitted to access directly, they could put the query in at one end, and look at the results at the other end. We might think of it as a cultural heritage or research version of 'Open Safely', the secure analytics platform for NHS electronic health records.[39] Such data is of course highly sensitive, yet it is still possible for users to run analytics without compromising its security.

Models for this kind of humanities infrastructure already exist. We might look for example to Hathi Trust, which has what is known as their 'non-consumptive use research policy'. This provides users with access to their data sets through three options: (1) web-accessible data analysis and visualisa-tion tools; (2) derived downloadable data sets; or (3) its data capsules – a system that grants a user access to a virtual machine which is a dedicated, secure desktop environment (called a 'Capsule') that exists within the Hathi Trust's secure compute environment.[40] These options may not include the free-reign access to data that researchers desire, but they are the next best thing.

Thankfully the UK's Arts and Humanities Research Council has made infrastructure for cultural heritage and research a priority over the next ten years, so there is reason to be hopeful that we are moving into an era where these challenges can be addressed by the community.[41] It is the topic we turn to in our next section.

3 Infrastructure

Digital projects rely on the foundations of good infrastructure: the systems and services that an organisation uses to work effectively. If the software or com-putational environment does not already exist, it must be built on the project, which is an additional workflow that must be designed and resourced with the correct expertise. This section draws on the particular experiences of LwM to consider the infrastructure required to support scholarship with digitised cul-tural heritage collections, both at the level of the individual project as well as at the national level. It looks at the role of access and storage in guaranteeing security and fulfilling data-sharing agreement requirements, but also considers how enhanced systems of security can complicate data access. Similarly, we look at the choices made in terms of data analysis and preprocessing, and how a well-implemented infrastructure can resist the hardest shocks and enable remote collaboration.

We will also share some of the lessons we have learned. The current system requires that individual projects such as ours spin up their own infrastructure and the lack of financial support to maintain it after the end of a project means that infrastructure is then closed down. In consequence, none of the labour and

---

[39] See www.opensafely.org/.   [40] See www.hathitrust.org/htrc_ncup.

[41] See www.ukri.org/blog/arts-and-humanities-infrastructure-enabling-knowledge-with-impact/.

knowledge is carried over into other research projects. It is a poor return for national investment and one worth rethinking along national lines, both in terms of human infrastructure (research software engineers familiar with working on humanities data) and the e-infrastructure needed to store and process large-scale cultural heritage and humanities research data.

3.1 Defining 'Infrastructure'

Developing 'infrastructure' sounds simple, but what does it mean in practice? Definitions vary. In digital scholarship, 'infrastructure' can represent services, workflows, data storage and computational or analytical facilities, each of which may be designed for either temporary or long-term use. Furthermore, as Susan Leigh Star points out, infrastructure is both relational and ecological, meaning different things to different groups, and inseparable from 'the balance of action, tools, and the built environment'.[42]

UKRI, the non-departmental public body of the government that oversees funding research, provides a definition of Research and Innovation Infrastructure that includes large-scale physical research facilities, equipment and sets of instruments (such as synchrotrons and research ships), networks of technologies and e-infrastructures (including data and computing systems and communication networks), and knowledge-based resources (including scientific, cultural, and artistic collections and archives).[43] This section largely works with UKRI's definition of infrastructure as networks of technologies but also considers 'ecological' questions of the training, knowledge, and expertise needed to design, implement, manage, and use infrastructure in research.

Our project had some unique requirements for infrastructure. In common with most digital humanities projects, we knew we would be working with large amounts of data. Less common, though, was the wide variety of forms that our data took: newspapers, maps, and census returns, amongst others. With each different data set we were faced with different data access and security requirements, and these in turn complicated infrastructural questions. Furthermore, our questions were open and exploratory. Our project was consciously designed as an experiment in building radical collaboration, and we planned to develop precise research questions to be built iteratively through the collaboration process, which meant that infrastructure could not be fully defined in advance in the usual way.

Broadly projects will need to consider the following steps, which are outlined in more detail below:

---

[42] Star (1999).   [43] See www.ukri.org/research/infrastructure/.

1. Where will the data be stored and analysed, and will this meet the project requirements?
2. As a sub-requirement, how will the data be made secure in line with the stipulations of data providers?
3. What pre-steps are required before the acquired data is ready for analysis?

Additional steps will be project-specific. One example from LwM was the process of linking data across different data sets. Because this challenge is one that may well be encountered by other projects and is being considered as part of various initiatives in the United Kingdom and elsewhere to create national collections of cultural heritage and humanities research data, we also outline our experiences in this section.

3.2 Data Storage and Computer Facilities

Before they embark on any work to secure data, projects need first to determine where they will put their data, and whether that environment is suitable for the kinds of analysis they need to undertake. Some project teams might have access to on-site high-performance computing (HPC) facilities through their institutions. The other option is employing a Cloud Compute solution. Decisions here will have implications across a range of domains, such as server capacity, access, usability, cost, and security. One that multi-institution collaborations will frequently face is the issue of access for the full team. The Alan Turing Institute is a national institute designed specifically to bring together researchers in data science and AI from across UK universities, and they are located in central London where they do not have space for big servers, so they have taken the pragmatic decision to utilise cloud computing facilities on their projects. Readers may be most familiar with Amazon Web Services (AWS); the Turing uses a similar service provided by Microsoft called Azure.

Employing an off-the-shelf cloud computing system offers a number of advantages. Commercial solutions like Azure are useful for handling large data sets at scale with minimal development, which should theoretically result in more efficient use of project time. Azure also provides managed access to data from anywhere the team may be working, with minimal installation and maintenance overhead requirements. Working with files and tools in the same system removes the limitations of space and bandwidth for working on data, a paramount concern when working with such large data sets. Researchers do not need to configure their own development environment, enabling easier access to data. Another key benefit was that it aided the delivery of data by institutions and companies outside the project: there are scripts to transfer data that avoid the circulation of shared disks and avoid insecure data transfers.

The benefits of cloud platforms explain why they are increasingly used, but this also exposes their vulnerabilities: when Netflix and everything else you like go down at the same time, chances are that AWS is down. Another downside is cost. As costs are charged according to storage and usage, cloud computing can be more expensive than on-premise computing; in particular, as these costs can be opaque to the individual user, making it easy to run up a large bill accidentally. More significant for us, however, were the complex questions of data security raised by our use of Azure.

Each of our data providers had a set of requirements about how their data should be stored, who should have access to it, and by what means. As discussed in Section 2, some data sets were completely open, while others were restricted in whole or in part due to commercial sensitivities, copyright, or the inclusion of data with personal names, most commonly bracketed by 'safe dates'. This was enshrined in the legal agreements that we entered into on receipt of data sets, which determined not only how team members could access the data, but also the extent to which the project could share that data or its derivatives alongside our project outputs.

Moreover, data security is crucially shaped by the institutions in which we are embedded. In our case, being based at the Turing meant that we were in a position to be informed by latest developments and best practices in data security within the data science and AI community, though along with this came a high-level expectation to model those best practices even when they are still at an emergent stage. Running our infrastructure through the Turing also meant that some BL collections were effectively 'third party' data. In this case, the Turing proposed that we should deploy a 'safe haven' for the storage of our data, in keeping with their newly drafted security tier classification system.

3.3 The Turing Data Safe Haven

The Turing Data Safe Haven was conceived in 2019 when a team of researchers at the institute (including three members of our project team) published a paper entitled 'Design choices for productive, secure, data-intensive research at scale in the cloud', which presented a policy and process framework for secure environments deployed in the cloud as software-defined infrastructure for productive data science research projects at scale.[44]

The Turing Data Safe Haven is designed to provide control over the following aspects of data security: data classification, data ingress, data egress, software ingress, user access, user device management, and analysis environments. Within these controls, the Turing Data Safe Haven project defines the

---

[44] Arenas et al. (2019).

roles, the steps and the processes to follow to ensure safe and secure data set acquisition. The policy prescribes the classification of data into five categories, depending on its level of sensitivity, and a corresponding set of security controls that characterise a safe haven suitable for handling data at each level. These levels are referred to as security *tiers*, ranging from Tier 0 to Tier 4. A Tier 0 environment is appropriate for data that are publicly available, or which are intended for immediate publication. At the opposite end of the scale, a Tier 4 environment is used to handle personally identifiable information where disclosure poses a substantial threat to personal safety, security, or health. This includes commercial or governmental data which may be subject to attack by sophisticated, well-resourced and determined actors. Tiers 0 and 1 are equivalent to a standard Azure virtual environment, with access to the wider internet and the ability to install external software. Higher, more secure Tiers have more limits, including disabling internet access (from Tier 2), and limiting inbound connections to dedicated machines (from Tier 3) and to specific, secure rooms (in Tier 4).

To determine the level of security needed for a data set, a series of questions are independently answered by a number of stakeholders, including the project team, the data owners (or a designated stand-in), and a third party (should there be a discrepancy between the outcomes the first two stakeholders reach). To give one example, as a result of this process, the British Newspaper Archive, which is a commercial product owned by the genealogy company FindMyPast, was classified as a Tier 3 data set owing to its commercial sensitivity. This might seem unnecessarily restrictive given that the material is more than 100 years old. However, the concern here is the impact of any inadvertent release of such data into the public sphere. Given this collection is key to FindMyPast's business model, the consequences for the provider could be severe. Most agreements would require the organisation storing the data (in this case the Turing) to be financially and legally responsible for any unauthorised release/ access, hence the need for the Data Safe Haven rating.

The policies and frameworks outlined above were not in place at the time that we drew up our funding bid or initial work plans, as they were drawn up and published in 2019. Nevertheless, as one of the Institute's flagship projects, it was expected that we would conform to the paper's recommendations. As a result, we became one of the first test cases for the implementation of the Safe Haven project at the Institute and the first long-running project to rely on it extensively.

Being a test case meant ironing out some kinks in the Tier model. The Safe Haven policy was designed around the security issues arising from working with national security and health data, rather than cultural heritage collections.

The Turing Safe Havens had been tested on short-duration projects with data requirements that were known in advance, limited in scale and not subject to change. The needs of a project spanning several years, with heterogeneous data from multiple providers and whose acquisition (and selection) was necessarily an ongoing process, called for the development of new techniques for data ingress and egress. Working through these issues required establishing a healthy and productive relationship with the Safe Haven team and the Turing IT department, which in turn created a substantial workload that was not calculated in our original work allocations for the research software engineers. Time not only equals money, it takes staff away from other tasks.

Employing the Safe Haven also threw up some unexpected difficulties when it came to linking data from different data sets. One of the key aims of the project (discussed further in Section 3.6) was to develop ways of linking heterogeneous data sources, such as newspapers, census data, directories, and maps. However, various agreements with each of these separate data owners resulted in data sets being assigned to different Tiers, which effectively put them in different boxes. This not only made linking more technically difficult, but it also required careful (and lengthy) negotiation of the different legal agreements determining the ways in which data can be stored, processed and shared. Solving these problems required some creative thinking. Above all, however, solving security challenges carried unanticipated time commitment. We would therefore recommend to other projects using data with security requirements to budget time generously for the acquisition and ingestion of that data.

3.4 Data Structure and 'Preprocessing'

Addressing rights issues and ingesting data into an appropriately secure environment are necessary steps for any data-driven humanities project. However they are not, in themselves, always sufficient for researchers to start undertaking analysis. Before data can be analysed one further step is very often necessary: preprocessing. We use this term instead of 'data cleaning' because of the way that term, as Katie Rawson and Trevor Muñoz have pointed out, has become 'a stand-in for longer and more precise descriptions of what people are doing in the initial phases of data-intensive research'. Rather we wish to highlight how preprocessing is a 'consequential step in the research process'.[45]

Preprocessing represents the preliminary processing of data before its intended use. Its aim is to understand the information contained in a data set, possible inconsistencies and their reasons (such as contemporary errors in digitisation or data management, or historical issues with missing or ambiguous

---

[45] Rawson and Muñoz (2019).

records), the format, and the data model used to represent information. Based on this information, data is mapped to the required data structure and manipulated as necessary for the required tasks. For example, some of our data were deposited in a 'blob storage' container in Azure, where it could be manipulated before ingesting it into a database.

It is often said that 80 per cent of data science is 'data cleaning', and our project certainly drew attention to this often neglected aspect of data-intensive research. We worked with multiple data types: textual data (e.g. newspapers), tabular data (e.g. census data), spatial data (e.g. metadata from map or newspaper collections), images (e.g. scanned maps and newspaper articles), and GIS data (e.g. vector data extracted from maps) and the preprocessing requirements of each varied considerably. Some were exceptionally well prepared for research and almost ready to go once in our systems; others were not. Undoubtedly though, the fact that we were working across so many data types added to our workload.

Some examples may make this more concrete. Textual data, for example, comes in a variety of different formats including XML, plain text, JSON, and proprietary formats such as Word documents. Data types for a specific collection type, such as newspapers, may vary over the decades. Today the most common standard for newspapers is a combination of METS/XML and ALTO/XML, but older data sets have been created using different standards, and even subtle differences across different schema or schema versions can impact the database architecture and database extraction.[46] So textual data is not *simply* textual data: one format can be preferable for database ingest or query (XML, text or JSON), one model can be better suited to capture textual nuances (TEI for manuscripts, DocBook for books), and another may simply have been more commonly used at a specific point in time. Whatever the reason, when the material is obtained, all the differences have to be taken into consideration when trying to use it as a single corpus. Different pre/post-processing pipelines have to be developed to store the material consistently in a database – and most importantly to be able to create links across pieces of content.

Similarly, spatial data can come in different formats: vectors (points, lines, and polygons), raster files (a grid of pixels), geographical attributes (additional information that describes specific features), geographic coordinates, and in variously structured data sets. We used both scanned maps and structured data with geospatial attributes, such as Wikidata and historical gazetteers (indexes of place names) – all of which needed preprocessing. Simply retrieving map

---

[46] Beals and Bell (2020), *The Atlas of Digitised Newspapers and Metadata* reveals the variety of metadata available across ten different newspaper databases.

images is a nontrivial task. The task is made easier by what is known as a tile server, a service that generates rendered images, or tiles, from a server. However, very few institutions make georeferenced maps available via such a service. We were fortunate to work with the National Library of Scotland's collection of digitised Ordnance Survey maps via their tile server (we received ~5TB of map sheets from them on hard drive, and have access to a much larger quantity of data via the tile server). When we digitised additional maps to supplement this data set, preprocessing steps were required to make the new scans research ready. These include linking scans to their item-level metadata, georeferencing, and demarcating areas outside the neat line (e.g. the boundary separating page borders from map content).

As should be clear, this preprocessing work calls for significant human and computational resources. Ideally, 'pipelines' that link preprocessing steps together should be flexible enough to accommodate different data formats. In reality, establishing this flexibility requires collecting samples of each probable type of data before designing the infrastructure. The more changes can be reduced and managed by early analysis of sample data, the better for the stability of the infrastructure.

Another key lesson regards the allocation of the responsibility for this preprocessing. When data is being passed between different institutions and people it is not always clear who is responsible for each step. Mapping people against the preprocessing steps required will help surface the existence of 'magic elves', wondrous creatures who can lurk within processes that everyone assumes will be done by someone else. Explicitly articulating the resources required for each step helps banish these magic elves.

Some researchers may expect to receive data perfect for their needs directly from a digitisation studio, and others will want (or expect) to pass the preprocessing step off onto their more technical colleagues. This may be necessary when the data wrangling is complex. However, the assumption that preprocessing is a kind of pre-work must be challenged. It conveys a value judgement, positioning it as an annoying pre-step before the 'real' work starts. But this is not the case; it is a valuable part of the research pipeline, and of value for projects and initiatives following, who can hopefully make use of the resulting data sets. Within the project too the process is crucially valuable in knowing what your data looks like, and understanding how it will be manipulated – what will be lost or added, where ambiguity may harden into certainty – before it is analysed in a specific research context. It is important for *all* team members to understand the decisions that are made at this stage, and how they might affect outcomes downstream. We therefore recommend spreading this stage as evenly as possible across the team, depending on skills and training available. We also suggest teams need to think about how credit flows for this kind of work (see Section 4). However, more work remains to be done within the context of universities and evaluation systems (such as the UK's Research Excellence Framework) before this work is valued as it should be.

3.5 Accessing and Analysing Data

One of our key requirements of our infrastructure was that it would facilitate collaboration between data scientists, historians, curators and library professionals, computational linguists and others. This meant that we not only wanted infrastructure with high-level processing power, but which also provided the ability to play with outcomes and to run smaller queries in ways that were accessible to members of the team with less technical backgrounds. Thinking this problem through itself requires a collaborative approach. Although the high-level computational analysis required by the project has not been implemented and run by historians, the research questions leading to development of pipelines and methods were developed in collaboration. This again brings us to the very human aspect of infrastructure: questions of training, and their impact on the choices that teams will make regarding programming languages, interfaces, and software used.

When working on a multidisciplinary digital project it can be hard for team members to communicate clearly given that historical and linguistic understanding and the most sophisticated technical skills are not equally shared by all members of the team. As we discussed in Section 1, following the work of Peter Galison on 'trading zones', it is vital to develop common 'contact languages', and we used a variety of training sessions, reading groups and meeting spaces in order to do so. To this, however, we must add the value of practising by doing. As team members came together to look at and manipulate the actual data, we began to forge a shared understanding of its qualities and of its power to address specific research questions.

In order to facilitate team-wide engagement with the data, however, it is often necessary to use or build platforms that use intuitive graphical user interfaces (GUIs). As Nils Reiter, Jonas Kuhn, and Marcus Willand have observed, GUIs frequently play a role in the planned workflows of DH projects, 'often tailored to the specific needs and research data of the project' so that scholars from different backgrounds are able to access data and investigate their research questions empirically via GUIs without additional training.[47]

---

[47] Reiter et al. (2017).

Inevitably, the use of GUIs throws up challenges as well. If users do not understand the basics of the operations happening under the hood then they are at risk of misinterpreting results, especially if they are not familiar with how to 'read' quantitative results. It is then essentially functioning like a black box, which does not increase knowledge in the ways we intended. The development of such interfaces also places an additional burden on the technical members of the team, as developing GUIs takes time, especially when they are part of an iterative research process, where data is explored, questions developed, and methods enriched and improved at each stage. If questions emerge gradually throughout the research process, the GUI may also need updating throughout the project. This can feel like wasted labour if it will not be hosted beyond the end of the project.

In our specific case, we did not plan to develop polished interfaces for end users due in part to the lack of funding support for hosting of such products beyond project end dates, but also because we were committed primarily to producing cutting-edge research – you cannot do *all* the things. We thought at some length about abandoning GUIs altogether. Some of the team held an ideological position that all users of the data should engage with it through the command line to understand its messiness and affordances in full. In reality, we realised we needed a range of approaches that met different team members at their skill level, and allowed us to progress. We therefore combined a number of freely available off-the-shelf GUIs for tasks like annotation and visualisation (to save on development time), with bespoke 'Jupyter Notebooks',[48] alongside custom code and scripts operationalised by the more computationally-skilled members of the team.

Jupyter is an open-source community that supports accessibility and trans-parency in data science by providing infrastructure and tools across a broad spectrum of use cases and programming communities. One of its most well-known projects is an interactive web tool known as a Jupyter Notebook, an interface in which researchers can combine software code, computational output, explanatory text and multimedia resources in a single document. Jupyter Notebooks have become part of a standard data science toolkit because they are embedded in a community of enthusiastic developers and are compat-ible with 'dozens of programming languages' including Julia, Python and R.[49] The Jupyter interface makes it easy to share, run and reproduce Notebooks. They can also be integrated easily with storage solutions (Azure in our case), and the document-like interface makes them less daunting to less tech-savvy researchers. For these reasons they have been used by cultural heritage

---

[48] For a similar combinatorial solution, see Melgar-Estrada et al. (2019).   [49] Perkel (2018).

institutions to provide accessible and transparent 'worked examples' of how to use digitised collections and metadata.[50] Most importantly, for us, it was relatively straightforward to provide training for historians and others on how to work with this kind of interface.

As part of the training supplied to the wider team in using Notebooks, we made the decision to teach people the basics of Python and to make that our language of choice. Multidisciplinary projects necessarily bring together people with different knowledge and expertise and also with different programming habits. Some people may be comfortable in several programming languages, while others may only know one well. Projects may choose to work mostly in one language or allow people to use any language that suits the task at hand. We settled on Python because it is a general-purpose language with very good software libraries for data analysis. In some rare circumstances other specialist languages or tools were used, such as Observable Notebooks for visualisations in JavaScript, or work in the language R by a collaborator building on other work in that language. But being a largely one-language project allowed us to spin-up and re-use Notebooks and other pieces of code in a much more agile way.

In addition to their use in running analysis, we employed Jupyter Notebooks to build *ad hoc* annotation tools to enrich data sets and enable data linkage, which facilitated the broad team to be involved more fully throughout the research pipeline. For example, in our work with the Ordnance Survey maps we developed an annotation setup embedded in a Jupyter Notebook, which can be seen in Figure 2. In this workflow the maps were broken down into smaller regions known as *patches*. As we can see in the figure, a patch is presented to the annotator (the top map image), alongside a contextual cue which includes the larger sheet of which it is a section (the lower map image), and the annotator then selects a label from user-defined options such as 'rail space' or 'no rail space' (the green or blue clickable options at the top of Figure 2). Once we accumulated a statistically significant number of labelled patches of maps, we could use that data to train a computer vision model to detect other patches containing visible rail infrastructure.[51] The interface is simple enough for historians on the team with little to no technical background to actively participate in the annotation process. We would therefore strongly recommend Jupyter Notebooks as an excellent option for other digital projects.

However, often (and increasingly) there will be off-the-shelf tools that will do many of the things that you need in a project. It is important to thoroughly survey

---

[50] See, for example, https://glam-workbench.net/; https://github.com/BL-Labs/Jupyter-notebooks-projects-using-BL-Sources; and https://data.cervantesvirtual.com/glam-jupyter-notebooks.

[51] For more on this work, see Hosseini et al. (2021).

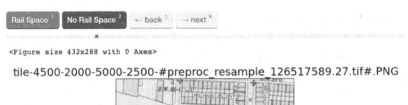

```
<Figure size 432x288 with 0 Axes>
```

tile-4500-2000-5000-2500-#preproc_resample_126517589.27.tif#.PNG

```
--------------------
Additional info:

URL to the NLS map: https://maps.nls.uk/view/126517589
```

Figure 2 Example of the annotation interface in *MapReader* pipeline for a 'rail space' experiment

existing solutions as they can save a project much time. For example, on the project we used a range of existing tools and platforms, including the crowdsourcing platform Zooniverse;[52] the semantic annotation platform INCEpTION,[53] and the geospatial analysis tool kepler.gl.[54] Thanks to their accessible and intuitive interfaces, thorough documentation, and support offered, applications like these help teams like ours to deliver results quickly, and explore data in ways that support the iterative nature of our research, without the overhead of setting up

---

[52] See www.zooniverse.org/.   [53] See https://inception-project.github.io/.
[54] See https://kepler.gl/.

systems from scratch. For example, we chose the Zooniverse platform so that we could develop crowdsourcing projects that engaged the public with our project without needing to write or host specialist software. By working with this established community we have been able to engage with over 2000 volunteers to date.

However, in some cases, our data – especially our newspaper corpus – was too big to manipulate using tools such as these, or required compute power that was beyond their capacity. In this case we made the decision to work with *defoe*, a digital text-mining toolbox, first developed at University College London and Edinburgh University with BL collections under the direction of Melissa Terras;[55] as some of the team overlapped with our project, using *defoe* made sense. There were a couple of benefits to working with this toolbox. Firstly, size and speed: *defoe* uses the power of analytic frameworks such as Apache Spark, Jupyter notebooks, and HPC environments to manipulate and mine huge digitised archives in parallel at great speed via a command line.[56] This is especially beneficial if you have access to top HPC, as we did briefly at the beginning of the project (Cray Urika-GX system, a high-performance analytics cluster with a pre-integrated stack of popular analytics packages, hosted at the University of Edinburgh by EPCC, and made available at that time for use by Turing researchers).[57] The second benefit was it had already been built, and that we had (at the outset at least) several team members who were familiar with it, and could therefore employ it with confidence.

While there are definite benefits to not having to build everything from scratch, using external systems means people have to learn to use yet another set of tools, or work in yet another environment. This is a consideration that each project will need to make for itself, balancing the availability of existing infrastructure, the size of the data, and the expertise available to them. In our case a subsequent change in personnel, coupled with some difficulties integrating Apache Spark into the Azure infrastructure, meant that *defoe* was not used in some stages of the project. We felt we did not have enough people with the relevant expertise to grapple with those particular technical challenges, and other research priorities meant that we focused on other solutions. However, we returned to *defoe* when specific needs around the processing of our newspaper corpora arose. We were grateful to have a range of solutions at our disposal to swap in and out as our priorities evolved.

---

[55] Terras et al. (2018).   [56] Filgueira et al. (2019).
[57] This was not a sustainable solution due to the fact that the Urika platform was end of life, and did not meet the security requirements for the Institute and our data providers.

3.6 Connecting Data

Many projects will work with just one data type and therefore have fairly streamlined infrastructure requirements. Working with multiple data sets means not only considering the infrastructure required for those data types, but also considering whether they need to be linked, what benefits this might bring, and how such linking might be done. While linking data was a specific aspiration of our project based on the kinds of multidimensional questions we were asking, the technical challenge is one that is important in the context of both national and international developments: various nations are investing in initiatives that are seeking to link their cultural heritage collections in order to break them out of individual institutional data silos.[58] Because of its importance for unlocking research, it is worth dedicating some attention to here.

A preparatory approach that we would recommend before even scoping work in such an area is the development of a 'metamodel'. For us this metamodel was a conceptual data model created on the basis of existing data models, while also taking into account the research agendas of our team members and methods we hoped to employ. Its ultimate goal was to conceptually visualise the characteristics and relationships between information included in different data sets.

A simple way to explain the usefulness of a linked data approach and how the metamodel might help is to consider *place*: the ways we might want to bring multiple sources to bear on a study of a particular locale. *Place* will be expressed differently in textual, tabular, or spatial data: it can be a simple name; it can have geographical coordinates associated with it; it can be expressed as a vector or a raster file. With a metamodel we can abstract this notion of *place* and describe it with the characteristics present in all different manifestations of such an entity, both the essential and the optional. Understanding how the different characteristics can be joined together should then make it possible to 'define' *place* and therefore enable data linkage across data sets. To take an example: we can extract the place of publication of a newspaper from its metadata, we can then attempt to link it to a place gazetteer and enrich it with geographical coordinates. If we then have georeferenced maps we can locate this place on a map using such coordinates. We can do the same process with train stations, birth places listed in census data, and so on and ultimately visualise all this information on the same maps to bring to light new patterns and potential research questions. As such, a metamodel is about finding a way to model concepts using all the

---

[58] See, for example, Europeana (www.europeana.eu/en) and the UK's Towards a National Collection (www.nationalcollection.org.uk/).

information available, as well as promoting the integration of research activity and the interoperability of software and data to avoid work becoming siloed. It also attempts to respond to theoretical questions in a pragmatic way.

The process in our project comprised two main phases: analysis and modelling. In the analysis phase we surveyed and analysed the data available, collected research agendas and interests, and looked at the most widely used data standards available. The proper modelling phase was based on sketching a conceptual model that would cover all the sources available. The goal was to incorporate the most relevant and successful features of existing standards and frameworks while remaining at a fairly high level within a sweet spot on the scale of abstraction; capturing the fundamental nature of the various entities of interest and the relationships between them without attempting to impose a rigid, overarching ontology. This work also included identification of the transformation that would be applied to the data, including input data, a description of the transformation or modification, and the outputs. The result was the model that allowed us to conceptualise the sources and transformations for entities such as a 'digitised document', 'named entity' or 'annotation', as demonstrated in Figures 3–5.[59]

The practical step of actually linking data was a separate challenge. Entity linking, the task of mapping a mention of an entity in text to its corresponding entry in a knowledge base, is an integral component of many text-mining applications. Linked data enables more sophisticated semantic querying and analysis of data. Existing entity linking systems tend to assume that the target term is always present as a name variation of a specific entity in the knowledge base, ignoring the elephant in the room: the high degree of potential variation in named entities. This is particularly pronounced with historical data, where variation may result from typographical errors, regional or diachronic spelling variation or, far too often, OCR-induced errors. To address this challenge we developed DeezyMatch, an open-source, user-friendly software library that precisely and efficiently addresses this often-overlooked component of the entity linking pipeline, which can be seamlessly integrated into existing linking tools, or as a component within a future infrastructure for linking collections data at scale.[60] It can mitigate the impact of name variation (including errors introduced by automatic text transcription) in entity linking and record linkage tasks, which are methodological aims of our project. We hope the development of this tool will allow more people to pursue projects using multiple collections or data types without needing first to develop infrastructure components.

---

[59] See Hobson and Tolfo (2019).   [60] Hosseini et al. (2020).

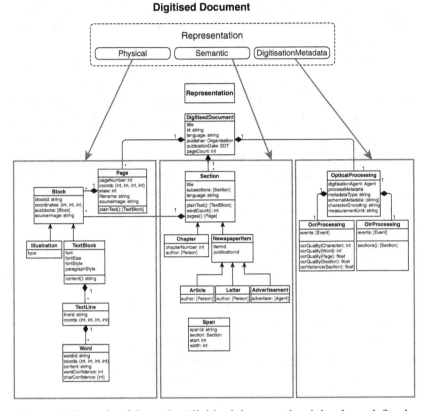

Figure 3 Example of the entity 'digitised document' as it has been defined in the metamodel

The utility of a tool like DeezyMatch can be demonstrated by the development of one of the first linked data sets we produced on the project: our Structured Timeline of Passenger Stations in Great Britain (StopsGB), which uses Michael Quick's reference work *Railway Passenger Stations in Great Britain: a Chronology,* which lists over 12,000 stations.[61] Being published originally as a book, this resource was not well suited for systematic linking to other geographical data. We transformed this into an openly available structured and linked data set using DeezyMatch to determine the best matching entity from Wikidata candidates for each station.

Linking tasks such as this are complicated, however, by the different data agreements imposed on different data sets. These can present a challenge not only in terms of the environment in which one can undertake analysis but also the extent to which linked data sets can be shared at the end of the process for use by

---

[61] Coll Ardanuy et al. (2021).

Named Entities

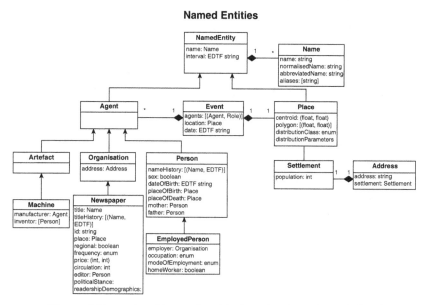

Figure 4 Example of 'named entities' as they have been defined
in the metamodel

others. An example of this is the full census (I-CeM: SN 7856) data set containing all the names and addresses, discussed previously in Section 2. Because this was covered by a special licence that required a high level of security, we theoretically needed to undertake this work in the more restrictive Safe Haven environment (Tier 3), which makes creative and iterative development harder and creates a data set that cannot be fully shared at the end. It is an issue that needs to be carefully considered by those seeking to work on multiple data sets with similarly restrictive terms and conditions.

Based on our experience, we would make two recommendations to allow for agile development of methods, and for sharing outcomes in terms of both methods and data. Firstly, to allow for data to be linked and analysed in a lower security tier (i.e. still secure but not requiring review of every bit of code going into that environment) we suggest making a new version of the data that meets the demands of that less restrictive environment. This could be a derived data set: so with our FindMyPast newspaper data this might be a set of Ngrams. Alternatively, one could make a new version of the data that strips out the sensitive material. For example, in the case of the I-CeM special licence data we created a new version that included the street name, but stripped out the street numbers and created a hash for the person's name that could not be linked back to the full census data. This allowed us to then link those street names to our other geo-coded data and more easily analyse it.

Annotations

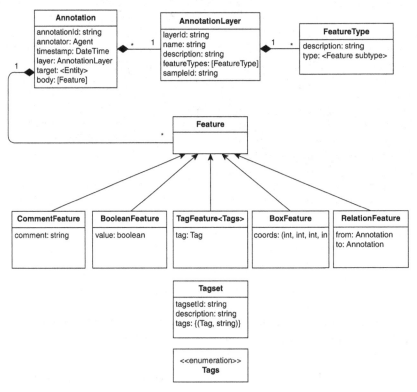

Figure 5 Example of the 'annotation' entity as it has been defined in the metamodel

However, this does not solve the issue of being unable to share that data freely. To address this we had identified an additional open data set, available through The National Archives, which is an index of street addresses that are cross-referred with the page numbers of the census.[62] Accordingly, when we want to release our Python package for geocoding historical census data, we will release two versions. The first can be used by teams who also have access to the special licence version of the census data (I-CeM: SN 7856). The second can be used with the openly-licensed street index, which will allow users to replicate some of what we have done. This is vital for reproducible research. This is also why we have also chosen to link our data to the re-usable OS Open Roads,[63] rather than the premium version which enables more fine-grained linking to individual

---

[62] The Historical Streets Project, details archived at UK Government Archive: https://webarchive .nationalarchives.gov.uk/ukgwa/*/http:/yourarchives.nationalarchives.gov.uk/.

[63] www.ordnancesurvey.co.uk/business-government/products/open-map-roads.

houses but compromises reproducibility. We would encourage teams to always choose the most open version of data possible and, where this is impossible, to find proxy data sets that others in the community might be able to use so that they can join the scholarly exchange.

3.7 Conclusions

The decisions a project makes about infrastructure must be pragmatic, and consider what is enough for the task in hand. Acquiring data samples as soon as possible in a project allows the team to understand requirements. Choices about secure data access necessarily add barriers to access that can create overhead to sketching ideas in code. Projects may want to consider the payoff between having the perfect data with restrictive requirements versus less ideal data that has free and permissive terms of use. Crucially, projects should build in much more flexibility and time to set up the infrastructure than they think they will need, as it is foundational work that can create problematic bottlenecks in workflows should data be delayed, or in a format that contains different preprocessing needs from those anticipated.

Our second message concerns the balance between reusing pre-existing tools and software versus building bespoke solutions. It is important to thoroughly survey existing solutions as they can save a project much time. However, there exists a tension between choosing tools – whether software suites, collaboration methods or programming languages – that are familiar, versus those that more precisely match a project's needs. While it can be tempting to turn to existing tools, or those that are already in use for other parts of the project to meet specific needs, this can mean trying to fit square pegs into round holes. Sometimes the biggest contribution you can make is adapting or developing a piece of software that meets the needs of a community of users.

A more serious problem, that we must return to here, is the immense effort of spinning up infrastructure at the beginning of a project, only to have to pack it away at the end. It is frustrating for the team, and it is a poor return on public money. We believe that while our advice above is useful in the current research environment, funders need to think strategically about the bigger picture to ensure that efforts are not reduplicated with every new venture. On the most modest scale, there need to be more funding schemes to support software and infrastructure created on projects beyond the grant period, and for promoting their re-use and adaptation. Ideally, however, digital projects would be served by a national infrastructure – whether it be a central or distributed system. Thankfully the UK's Arts and Humanities Research Council is already in the process of scoping what this entails for the arts, humanities and cultural heritage, and is planning how to resource this over the next decade. We hope that our recommendations in these pages can help inform the development of principles and standards. Specifically – as we hope our foregoing examples show – we would contend that the process of research is the only real test of how well imagined systems work against real data and research problems, and thus if scoped solutions serve the needs of the community. Infrastructure initiatives therefore need to be designed within a framework of application, testing, re-use, and iteration.

4 Radical Collaboration

Large digital projects have many moving parts: as we have seen in the previous two sections, obtaining data and building a functioning infrastructure are major pieces of work in their own right. However, underpinning all aspects of inter-disciplinary projects is the *human* infrastructure, and a project's success depends on it functioning to its full potential. *Living with Machines* was designed at the outset as an experiment in what we described as 'radical collaboration'. By this we meant a form of collaboration in which no discipline or professional practice was in service of another, and one in which we empowered all researchers to bring their expertise to the table. However, this is a difficult vision to bring to pass within the current model of higher education and research funding.

Universities, and funding councils, are, at heart, hierarchical organisations, and the traditional funded project is delivered through a hierarchical model, in which a team works through the preconceived vision of the Principal Investigator (PI) and Co-Investigators (Co-Is). By contrast, the Agile method-ology employed in the software design community (and discussed in Section 1) provides an alternative to the top down or 'waterfall' model.[64] Neither model, however, was designed with a large, publicly funded, interdisciplinary digital humanities project in mind, and so researchers in this field need to steer a middle way between the initial top-down design and the subsequent delivery of the project. Of course at its outset LwM *was* a project designed by a handful of senior investigators. Our challenge was to move to a more horizontal form of collaboration in light of the full expertise of the hired team.

As described in Section 1, in our first year we put considerable effort into the development of what Galison describes as new 'contact languages' and zones of exchange in the belief that cross-disciplinary understanding and communication would be required for effective collaboration. However, the building of

---

[64] See Thesing et al. (2021).

team-wide communication is not a one one-off act that can be 'ticked off' in the first year of the project, which is why we have returned to the topic of collaboration in the final section of this Element. Instead, it is an ongoing process that runs throughout the project and requires constant reflection and response as the project vision develops. Returning to Galison's framework of trading zones, there is no point investing time in allowing the wider research team to develop new interdisciplinary 'pidgin languages' and fully functioning 'creoles' if you are not going to harness these new ways of thinking and communicating.

This section is essentially about the transition from the start-up phase of a project into a stable endeavour in which all members are moving together forwards with a shared vision, despite the different experiences they bring. It is a transition that is known to be challenging regardless of the professional setting; it is perhaps no surprise that there is a popular literature in project management on the 'messy middle' of projects and business ventures.[65] Its aim is to suggest ways that allow a project to steer a clear path through the exciting mess created by new ways of working.

In the following pages we suggest some strategies that emerged from the experiences of LwM, a team of more than twenty individuals drawn from a variety of different occupational backgrounds and trained in radically different disciplinary traditions and one which changed and grew over time. These include the introduction of a defined work rhythm and a review process, that can act as a mechanism for evaluating and rethinking a project's intellectual concerns and its organisational structures and hierarchies as well as: developing a project Roadmap; adapting meeting culture to changing needs; keeping good project documentation; and ensuring that labour and intellectual credit is suitably distributed by agreeing a model of credit and authorship. In covering these topics, the section also engages with the impact of the Covid-19 pandemic – not only on our project but on work culture more widely. While some of these topics may sound like banal administrivia, we would contend that such frameworks are necessary to ensure that being radical does not lead to other power structures emerging in unforeseen ways.

4.1 Moving Forward

If a collaborative project is successful in the starting-up phase, the exchanges should be highly generative, and in our case they certainly were. As the first stage of our project drew to a close, we had a project workshop to review the research generated by each of the Labs. This workshop marked an important threshold in the project. While we have already discussed the benefits of the

---

[65] For example, Belsky (2018).

Minimum Research Outcome as a mechanism for creating shared project ideas and delivering proof-of-concept work (see Section 1), we want here to consider the *review process* that followed it.

At its simplest level, the workshop served as a moment to evaluate the intellectual achievements of the first stage of the project as each of the Labs presented their MROs. In the event, however, the outcome of the workshop went far beyond an evaluation of the work achieved to date and also touched upon a raft of questions regarding how we wished to collaborate as a team. The Labs, it is worth recalling, had been established before the full team was in place. This workshop therefore also presented the opportunity to reflect upon the Lab structure and question whether it still reflected the scope and ambitions of the project.

The team's consensus was that whilst clear connections were emerging between and across Labs, the Lab structure risked siloing the work that was conducted in them along more traditional disciplinary lines. Any large project will inevitably experience strong centrifugal forces working to spin sections off onto their own research path. Most scholars from the humanities are used to working if not entirely alone, certainly within very small teams, and have a natural inclination towards breaking off small tasks with small groups of people in order to get things done. Perhaps more significantly, however, was the fact the disciplinary differences between team members and across the Labs were immense. Our goal was radical collaboration, and our assessment at the end of the first year of the project was that the Lab structure risked not fully achieving that goal.

As we entered the second year of the project, therefore, we resolved to dissolve the Labs in favour of another structure, which we dubbed 'Strands'. The emphasis on intersecting interests, questions, and methods aimed to improve the integration of the different parts of the project. To put it metaphorically, Strands could be plaited more easily than Labs. This was a bold move, but one a well-structured review and workshopping process were able to achieve. The lesson we took from this was not to stay too wedded to initial frameworks but to be willing to restructure in response to better organising principles. In reality the Strands had a lot in common with the headings of the Labs, but they were organised around more focused topics and specific research questions rather than broader themes.

At the same time as dissolving the Labs, and breaking work down into smaller segments, we decided to work to a different rhythm. We concluded that the nine months we allocated for designing and reporting on the MROs were too long. The longer that small teams worked together, the harder it became for those outside to keep up with the work others were doing.

Furthermore, proceeding for such a long period risked allowing research to diverge in different directions and committing too much resource to something that was not working. We therefore resolved to break our future working stints into shorter cycles, of three rather than nine months, and make the review process a quarterly practice.

Moving to shorter work cycles not only helps to produce greater flexibility by breaking work down into smaller segments, but it also builds in a much more frequent cycle of review. This allows the broader team to stay abreast of the full gamut of activities being undertaken and provides a very refreshing punctuation that has enabled us the opportunity to pause and celebrate the progress that has been made. Sometimes when projects are so focused on all they want to achieve in the future, it is easy to forget how far they have come. It is good to store up these wins to sustain a team when progress may be slower, and when harder conversations might be required about how to prioritise activities going forward (which often means letting some things go).

Moving to a shorter work iteration also allowed us to build in more regular moments of rest and reflection. As we entered the second stage of the project, we instituted a two-week rest period after each work cycle, for people to use as they saw fit. This might involve tying up loose ends, planning for the next work iteration, working on a tangential idea, or just taking vacation. Their second function was to provide time and space for the team to think together about what had worked well, and what had worked less well in the previous work iteration, and try to figure out what could be done better next time. We experimented with a variety of formats for these self-reflections, sometimes through open conversations, and sometimes via anonymous writing sessions with question prompts. Several fields have developed retrospectives as an element of best practice here,[66] and they are a key part of Agile, but they are not common practice as yet in traditional humanities. We would recommend these as an important feature for any large-scale project because of the way it allows all project members to be heard, and for the project leadership to have the opportunity to continually make improvements to how the project is run.

Shifting from Labs to Strands and working to a shorter three-month cycle with built-in rest periods were fairly straightforward ways of improving the quality of our collaboration. But effective collaboration also required thinking how best to harness the talents and capacities of each team member. At the start of our first year, we were a fairly traditional team of PI and Co-Is, in established, sometimes quite senior, institutional positions. We mapped out the project

---

[66] Both gamestorming and liberating structures have activities designed for reflection. See, for example, https://gamestorming.com/actions-for-retrospectives/. www.liberatingstructures.com/26-generative-relationships-st/.

goals, drew up job descriptions, and recruited the team. By the end of the year, with postdoctoral and researcher positions filled, our team was larger, but it was also far more heterogeneous. How best to incorporate the insights and initiatives of those joining the project at an earlier stage of their career? How best to democratise intellectual decisions?

It is hard to find a balance between completely democratic decision-making (which risks creating a chaotic environment full of dead ends) and top-down management (which risks failing to harness the full potential of the team and sowing the seeds of discontent). We decided to experiment with a specific way of flipping the hierarchy: the idea was that members of the wider team would lead the work taking place under the new Strands of work, with the Investigators supporting and mentoring them in a way that also freed them up from administration to participate more actively in the experimental work, and to keep their eyes on the overarching picture. The shorter new three-month cycle allowed us to take this risk and reap its benefits. By making researchers owners of the work we enabled them to more actively shape the research agenda, and to give them opportunities to develop their leadership skills. We would strongly recommend this for interdisciplinary teams, as we found the results to push us to more radical forms of interdisciplinarity than we imagined at the outset.

In sum, we essentially took two risky moves one year into the project: to change and shorten the structure of work from Labs to Strands, and to democratise the management and delivery of work. Although we believe these shifts ultimately paid off, the transition was not easy: it took some time to communicate the new strategy, get buy-in, experiment with what that actually looked like in practice, and adjust our practices accordingly.

What we believe is required to negotiate through a phase change in a project like this is a Roadmap (or whatever name you chose to give it), setting out a clear plan of the project ahead, and who will deliver its constituent parts. For us, this was a clearly articulated vision of the goals of each of the different Strands, as well as of the relationships between them, in order that everyone knew what work was progressing and what fellow team members were working on at any given point in time. In such a document it is vital that all priorities and proposals are transparent, equal, and in line with the declared values of the project. In essence this constituted a more granular version of the Milestones and Deliverables with which we were able to update our delivery plan – in other words, supplementing the 'rules of exchange' articulated by that foundational document (see Section 1). Alternatively you might think of it as a pre-step to a Gantt chart, providing a longer narrative context and intellectual justification for each task.

If such a document is to reflect a change in intellectual ownership, its drafting also requires collaborative shaping. We would still recommend that investigators produce a skeleton structure, but thereafter that vision can be fleshed out in a collaborative process. In our case we asked all team members to share their thoughts about discrete research tasks they would like to conduct as part of the project, as well as their own relationship to that work – whether as leader, active contributor, or in a consultative role. Our Roadmap sought to crystallise emergent Strands into formal 'Work Packages' and sub-tasks. Under these headings we articulated the outcomes associated with each strand of work, whether as articles, books, code, data sets, tutorials, or engagement activities with the wider public. In the shorter term, the detail of these deliverables was much more clearly articulated; for the longer term, we granted ourselves more latitude by identifying the types of outcomes to which we aspired, with steps for adding more detail iteratively.

The benefit of such a document is not only better communication within the project, but a clear vision that aids communication beyond the project too. It provides a clear plan for distributed ownership, and ensuring the right balance of skills across the tasks. And it can be a generative way of ensuring that all the ideas for research outcomes are documented in one place. However, that generative function needs careful management, as it will almost certainly produce plans for considerably more work than can be completed. This is where a governing structure such as a Project Management Board is still needed: they will need to make decisions, sometimes rather difficult ones, about what work will move forward and when. The result of such a winnowing process will take the team closer to a more traditional Gannt chart. However this should not be set in stone, but iterated on during the quarterly review process, revisiting the priorities and deciding which tasks can no longer be completed, dropped, or perhaps hived off into a spin-off project.

The review process following the MRO, then, was an important turning point in the project. At this juncture, it was tempting to harness the enthusiasm of the team and press on with the exciting work evident in constituent parts of the team, and whilst we did this to some extent, we also took a moment to pause and to rethink the nature of our collaboration. To repeat: interdisciplinary research requires collaborative teamwork, but there is no blueprint for how large, complex and diverse teams actually do that. Our experience is that finding meaningful ways to collaborate is part of the intellectual work facing any large project. In other words, building in review processes and reflecting on how your team is functioning are as vital as getting on and doing the research.

No sooner had we laid out our plans, however, than the pandemic hit. Consequently, in addition to the inherent challenges in making a transition to a new work structure we needed to shift, and very quickly, from a team committed to in-person collaboration to one that conducted all elements of work online.

4.2 Moving Online

We entered Phase 2 with a new rhythm of work, a new team structure, and a new Roadmap to work to. But before our new systems could properly bed in, Covid-19 halted all physical meetings and brought a raft of new and unanticipated changes to our project. While these are specific to a very particular moment in history, the events of 2020 made many people evaluate the way they had been working, and we are unlikely to ever fully return to the way things were before. Therefore we believe it is worth reflecting on the experiences and lessons of this period, to document not only the barriers we faced but also the discoveries we made in the process about how teams can and should function

There can be no denying that the pandemic caused disruption to our project. The closure of our home in The Alan Turing Institute for several months was inevitably concerning for a project that was committed to radical collaboration and in-person working. Meetings were rapidly moved online, but the end of in-person meetings involved the loss of opportunities for casual conversations, which can play an important role in helping teams to function effectively. Unscheduled private conversations can play a large role in helping to support and mentor individuals or, conversely, to diffuse small conflicts and prevent disagreements from festering and escalating. We lost serendipitous encounters for learning, brainstorming and problem-solving that were more natural in physical spaces. We also encountered challenges in welcoming new team members, which had initially relied on the in-person immersion process of working side by side, as well as the more formal 'onboarding' process used by the institution. One important tool for trying to recreate these soft interactions was the use of an online messaging system (in our case Slack). Although some of the team had been slow to warm to this mode of communication when so much work was in person, during the turn to fully-online work we collectively adopted the platform as an informal team-wide channel of communication. It allowed quick queries to be dealt with swiftly, as well as for the team to share personal news. It is a mode of communication that has remained central even as some of the team have returned to in-person working.

Lockdowns also posed problems specific to our identity as a data-centric project, particularly concerning infrastructure, and data and content accessibility. An extra strain was placed on those involved in data acquisition, wrangling and infrastructure-building. For instance, the design and delivery of the Safe

Haven environment (discussed in Section 2) was complicated because higher Tiers originally required location-specific access. Rethinking this required additional work not just at the project level but also at the institutional level, with one person being pulled off our team for several months to fulfil this requirement across the Turing. We faced additional challenges around data acquisition, specifically in the case of our census data, where the terms of our access were linked to IP and physical premises at the Turing. The additional security measures required by the UK Data Service to enable off-premises access during the pandemic required additional work by the team. On a more mundane level, like so many other researchers we were affected by lack of access to physical books and papers.

Crucially, the closure of the BL during the first lockdown, and again in December 2020, meant that our digitisation of additional materials on the project was halted, and once it restarted it did so at a reduced rate. The project was thus forced to streamline its planned digitisation and set a deadline for when to stop bringing new data into the project. This decision, whilst difficult, had the benefit of freeing up some budget, which we sought permission from UKRI to use to extend and reprofile the grant to allow four months of additional funded time for all team members, which we hoped would make up in part for the disruption to work caused by the team's additional care responsibilities, illness, and the increased administrative burden caused by the need to renegotiate data access. This reprofiling process, of course, required considerable work in its own right, on the part of the PI, project manager, and Turing finance team. As with all of the above it shows the need for projects to be reactive and flexible in the face of unforeseen circumstances.

These disadvantages notwithstanding, we also came out of the pandemic with a number of positive improvements to our working methods in place. One permanent gain has been the imposition of greater control over the spiralling number of meetings. These had already begun to be challenging as they sprawled across the week, cutting into productive time. With the onset of the pandemic, several team members' time became even tighter. In order to accommodate home-schooling parents and the many part-timers on the project, we selected a fixed day for project meetings and established far-tighter central control over the scheduling of meetings. Entrusting our administrator with the responsibility for fixing team-wide meetings has helped to reduce the time spent by individual team members, reduce the incident of mistakes around scheduling and clashes, and enabled us to build a far more coherent calendar that works for all, regardless of whether they engage in-person or online.

The pandemic also caused us to reconsider our approach to Project Board Meetings for the PI and Co-Is. Pre-pandemic these had been scheduled relatively infrequently, just four a year. We relied on informal opportunities to chat and grab a coffee to discuss any issues that arose in-between times. With the loss of these opportunities, we realised we needed a more robust approach for all those responsible for the project to meet regularly – not least as the pandemic threw up a lot of extra work, such as reprofiling the budget and overseeing the team during a highly stressful period. We shifted our Project Board Meetings from quarterly to monthly, to serve the dual function of raking over the day-to-day business of running the project and managing workload and workflow, and to monitor progress and larger project milestones. More regular meetings also had the advantage of distributing decision-making between PIs and Co-Is more evenly, and thus bringing the governance in line with our preference for democratic and open working methods.

Moving online also offered some opportunities for us to interrogate our assumptions about how research can and should be undertaken, and to test new ways of collaboration, some of which have proved highly satisfactory. Remote working has proved a positive experience for focusing and saving on commuting time (and fatigue), particularly for Co-Is based outside London. Dissolving the distinction between on- and off-site has increased the sense of inclusion in the project for those who were not always able to participate in person, and levelled the playing field for people who have different accessibility requirements, or work flexible hours around caregiving and other activities. It has allowed those additional pressures on our lives to become more visible to our colleagues, which has only been a positive in terms of increasing empathy and team spirit.

We also introduced new styles of collaborative working. Team writing sprints or collaborative paper/code writing, in which team members sat individually on Zoom whilst working together on shared documents, proved particularly successful. Blocking slots of time to write papers collaboratively – a good way to protect time from being splintered by competing calls for our attention – was certainly one of the best decisions made by the team and will be continued throughout the rest of LwM, and as we scope future projects. When thinking about which activities should go back to being in person, we would say that these kinds of 'doing' activities would benefit most; administrative meetings can easily continue to be done online to save on travel.

One effect, that it is worth pausing to reflect on, was our renewed commitment to documentation. It is not a glamorous part of collaboration, but it is vital, and doubly important when collaborating remotely and often asynchronously. Other professional settings have been thinking about remote work for much longer and already have established norms. One example is GitLab's remote Manifesto. Of their nine values, it is notable that four of them are about documentation: writing down and recording knowledge (over verbal explanations); written processes (over on-the-job training); public sharing of information (over need-to-know access); opening up documents for editing by anyone (over top-down control of documents).[67] Cutting across these values, LwM and similar projects are likely to have four kinds of documentation they need to consider:

1. Central documents setting out the 'rules of exchange' such as the Project Charter, Delivery Plan, Roadmap, and records from end of iteration reviews, and so on;
2. Governance documents such as finances, risk register, reporting to the funder, and minutes of the Project Management Board;
3. Wider team-generated records and minutes of meetings;
4. Documentation of code.

While a small number of files may require restricted access due to their sensitivity, the keeping of such documentation is predicated on transparency, the ability to reconstruct decisions at a later stage, and to minimise any friction in the work process.

It is vital to have a plan for such documentation at the outset. On document types 1, 2, and 4, we had a good plan at the outset, and it was implemented satisfactorily for the running of the project. We had chosen a central repository for our central documents and governance documents (types 1 and 2); the project manager oversaw the latter, and the former were a full-team responsibility. Code documentation (type 4) benefited from there being established workflows in the research software engineer/data scientist constituency of our team, using GitHub. GitHub enables each workstream within a project to develop its own repository. These repositories can be private while code is being developed, then shared when the code is stable. A system of 'pull requests' allows people to edit existing code with a review process before changes are merged into the main body of code. When the repository is made public, all the previous work is also made public, so team members do need to be relatively comfortable working in the open. The values of open science on our project also meant that the teams behind the release of code were committed to ensuring it was fully documented before being publicly shared. In this case documentation means anything you write in addition to your code to help someone else understand how it works.[68]

Although GitHub is not optimised for project management, we have found that with the correct use of the different features it has (tags, milestones, referencing), it can do some of the work required for wider team-generated

---

[67] See, for example, GitLab (2015).
[68] For a guide to documentation best practices, see https://google.github.io/styleguide/docguide/best_practices.html.

records (type 3 above). As described briefly in Section 1, each Lab (and subsequently each task within a work package on the Roadmap) had its own project board in GitHub. Most boards share the same columns – to do, in progress, done – across which sub-tasks, known as tickets, are moved at the fortnightly sprint meetings. But the reasons for moving tickets across a board need to be recorded, not only for those not in the room but also in order that team members can recall those reasons months or years later. Before the pandemic, different Labs fulfilled this in different ways: sometimes none were made, sometimes they were stored on the central document repository, sometimes they were added as notes to individual tickets. Moving online made the need for transparent and retrievable documentation even more pressing. The scattering of documentation across different systems has made it difficult for new team members to find their way in the project at the beginning. We solved this with a simple tweak in phase two of the project, with an additional column being added to GitHub boards for minutes. In this respect, we found that GitHub offered a very flexible, customisable way to set up a project board. We would recommend that other large collaborative projects find similar mechanisms to ensure all processes and decisions are easily discoverable.

Overall the transition to remote working was achieved only through the labour and emotional effort of the entire team. Moreover, it is important to recognise that its effects have been, and will continue to be, unevenly distributed. In common with teams across the globe, the pandemic has forced us to reconsider some of our initial assumptions about how best to collaborate. We had underestimated some of the possibilities for, and indeed advantages of, remote working and incorporating new working patterns have been to the benefit of the project overall.

4.3 Authorship and Credit

Another issue that came to the fore as we entered the middle phase of the project concerned the flow of credit on our first project outputs. In the case of large projects where co-authorship will be common, this can be a sensitive issue that needs handling carefully to ensure that team members are fully valued for their work. This is an issue both of team morale and career progression because in many cases team members (especially those on fixed-term contracts) will need the right number and kinds of publications or other outcomes to ensure their future in the field. Of course, in the more traditional quarters of history departments, co-authorship is not common beyond acts of co-editing collections of essays, partly because large collaborative projects such as this have not been the norm in the past. On this project then we have had to look to fields in which co-authorship is more standard to inform our practice, and there are lots of helpful resources recommending best practice within different disciplinary contexts.

The question is not just about who gets their name on a list of authors, but also in which order they appear. In many scientific sub-fields the assumption is that the first author on a publication will be the 'primary thinker, doer, and writer behind the work'.[69] The last place is often given to the senior academic supervising the work. Historically this cultural practice led to scientists leading a lab to be automatically included in papers emerging from that lab, regardless of whether they made an intellectual contribution or not, in recognition of the other kinds of labour that go into running such a research environment (grant capture, management, supervision, etc.). However, many scientific journals now recommend in their submission guidelines that everyone listed as an author should meet their criteria for authorship. *PLOS One* (a journal that publishes across science, engineering, medicine, and the related social sciences and humanities) also makes the inverse case, that 'everyone who meets our criteria for authorship must be listed as an author'.[70] Their authorship criteria is based on the International Committee of Medical Journal Editors (ICMJE) Uniform Requirements for Manuscripts Submitted to Biomedical Journals, which lists four conditions for authorship credit that all authors must meet:

- Substantial contributions to conception and design, acquisition of data, or analysis and interpretation of data, and
- Drafting the article or revising it critically for important intellectual content, and
- Final approval of the version to be published, and
- Agreement to be accountable for all aspects of the work in ensuring that questions related to the accuracy or integrity of any part of the work are appropriately investigated and resolved.

The authors of the collaboratively authored *Turing Way* – a handbook for best practices in open and reproducible data science – point out how some journal policies on authorship force projects to make the distinction between contributors and authors.[71] While authors create the written work, there is a much broader hinterland of labour that goes into the production of data-driven and computational research. The need to better taxonomise and describe these different kinds of labour in scientific publications was behind the development of CRediT (Contributor

---

[69] See 'Ethical Research in Practice', www.authorshipethics.com/culture/.

[70] See 'PLOS ONE, Authorship', https://journals.plos.org/plosone/s/authorship.

[71] The Turing Way Community (2019).

Roles Taxonomy) which is a high-level taxonomy, including fourteen roles, that can be used to represent the roles typically played by contributors to scientific scholarly output. These are: Conceptualisation, Data curation, Formal Analysis, Funding acquisition, Investigation, Methodology, Project administration, Resources, Software, Supervision, Validation, Visualisation, Writing – original draft, Writing – review & editing.[72] Many scientific journals now expect contribution statements, and taxonomies help facilitate the writing of such statements.

The digital humanities have also been grappling with these issues for some time. In 2011 Adam Crymble initiated FairCite in an attempt to change authorship and credit practices in line with the changing landscape of humanities research. It argued that an intervention was needed because of the 'resistance in the humanities amongst principal investigators and administrators to the idea of extending "authorship" to "non-academic" staff, students, or contractors'.[73] Despite these calls being a decade old, there remains work to be done, as demonstrated by recent discourse on Twitter. In a thread in August 2021 Richard Jean So drew attention to a continuance of the practice of articles and books being issued with a single author that nevertheless rely on the computational work of graduate or undergraduate researchers.[74] Jacob Eistenstein pointed out that 'humanists don't understand how to credit, say, a student running a regression on data they have also processed because that labour itself is generally alien to the humanities. So the 'natural' default is to write it off as 'merely' a kind of RA work'.[75]

While it is reasonable for different fields to arrive at different conclusions about where the bar for authorship should be, our project settled on a more generous and inclusive model of authorship. While we had set out principles for credit in our project charter, in the process of producing our first article we realised that these values needed to be articulated as a clearer set of guidelines to avoid ambiguity. The resulting guidelines are informed by our team members' different scholarly backgrounds, the involvement of team members past and present with initiatives like *The Turing Way,* and by values set by colleagues that we admire, such as the authors of the Collaborators' Bill of Rights, which (like FairCite) recommends that the DH community should 'default to the most comprehensive model of attribution of credit'.[76] Our guidelines contain a list of values, as well as practical steps in the process of article conceptualisation, writing, and submission, which we share here as we think it could structure discussions on other teams.

---

[72] See 'Contributor Roles Taxonomy', https://credit.niso.org/.

[73] Fair Cite, http://faircite.wordpress.com. See Crymble et al. (2019).

[74] https://twitter.com/RichardJeanSo/status/1428038806276612106.

[75] https://twitter.com/jacobeisenstein/status/1428065340102115332.   [76] Clement et al. (2011).

Values:

- We want to credit all parts of the workflow in our publications and other outputs through authorship or citation of preceding outputs.
- Early publications will necessarily contain longer author lists due to the lack of preceding outputs to cite. If in doubt, we will always err towards generosity.
- All outputs should be regarded as open to anyone who wants to be involved, but author credit only comes with a substantive input in terms of conceptualisation, methodology, implementation, reproducibility, interpretation and analysis, data curation, software, visualisation, writing, and the labour of care undertaken through actively overseeing and managing a part of the project, where it materially helps a publication.
- In recognition of those different types of input, and to adhere to our values of collaboration and transparency, for publications we will employ the CRediT Taxonomy, for which we have built a 'film-credit' cover page for versions of our outputs deposited repositories. We will also seek to use the first footnote (or equivalent) in the published version of the paper to acknowledge this work division.
- We want to recognise the work that went into winning the grant through acknowledgement of PIs, Co-Is, funders and data providers on all outputs, but authorship credits will not be automatic. Rather, this needs to be based on the contribution made to that specific publication.
- Our decisions on authorship questions need to recognise the venue in which they are to appear, and the norms of publication in that field. But we also want to push on those norms, but not in a way that creates risk for those on the team on fixed-term contracts. This might mean shorter author lists in some venues (e.g. Humanities), and there we will seek to drive credit to others through generous citation, and acknowledgement notes.
- We acknowledge that the above may result in some awkward conversations, and we commit to getting better at these in the spirit of the project Charter!

Before you start a given output (article, code, data set, etc.)

- The task owner will facilitate these discussions, and likely be first or last author, depending on the field.
- Decide who are going to be authors, and who will take the lead, and take practical steps at the outset to ensure inclusion by emailing the entire LwM team and using the 'new publication' GitHub issue template. The task owner

will make the final decision of author inclusion, and any disputes will come to the Project Management Board.

- Our GitHub issue template will guide the process of including all key info in the early stage of publication planning. This ticket will be a 'home base' for the publication information, and an email will go out linking to the ticket for broader team awareness, and so those who wish to be involved have the opportunity.
- Be willing to revise the initial authorship plans if the balance of contribution to an article changes

During write up

- If anyone has defaulted to just commenting on the final draft, a conversation needs to be had about whether they wish to continue as author, or would better be credited as an internal reviewer in an acknowledgement.

At end

- Deal with any disputes in open conversation between all authors.
- We hope that this will never be necessary, but if it proves impossible to come to a consensual agreement the PI will arbitrate the case with two non-authors from the PMB (or, where appropriate due to conflict of interests, from elsewhere in Turing or advisory board), with one from the home discipline, and one from outside.

On code

- While we can see contributions (issues, Pull Requests, code pushes) if repos are open, they may not reflect the reality of those who contributed.
- We suggest adopting a taxonomy of contributions, for example, https://allcontributors.org/
- Extra marks for aligning the taxonomy across output types i.e. code and papers.

We have found these guidelines to be helpful in the planning phase of publications, and hope they might work for others too. We are especially proud of our film-style credit sheet that we have modelled for preprint versions deposited in repositories.[77] However, there have been tough conversations in negotiating how we do something radical on the project without sacrificing our early career colleagues for the benefit of the experiment. We feel this especially keenly for those seeking careers in

---

[77] For an example of this, see the Arxiv version of one of our earliest publications: https://arxiv.org /pdf/2005.11140.pdf, discussed in Nanni (2020), 'Highlighting Authors' Contributions'.

the humanities after the project, and how they will have to deal with the expectation of hiring panels, some of whom may be impressed by a quantity of multi-authored papers published in interdisciplinary venues, and others who will expect to see single-authored pieces in the most well-recognised venues in that discipline. We believe part of the role of our project is to challenge the more normative expectations, but our first responsibility is to the team members. Therefore, we have needed to plan carefully with our postdoctoral researchers in particular to ensure they are involved in a good mix of outputs: experimental multi-authored papers, tools, data sets and data papers, but also single-authored (or short-author list) interventions in the leading journals in their field. If compromises need to be made, our guiding principle is that it is the PI and Co-Is that should be making the compromise, as they are at a career stage where they can afford the gamble. Our project management board believes that one of our most important 'key performance indicators' (see Section 1) is the number of people in suitable employment following our project, and so our authorship policies seek to support that.

One key way that we are seeking to model new norms of authorship in the humanities is through the summative project book, which seeks to draw together the strands of research in one place. While a book is an unfamiliar kind of output for those in the sciences – and has therefore required some selling as a worthy use of time – it represents a shared goal that keeps in sight the need for the whole team to work together. While we have written above about the formation of work packages and sub-tasks as a mechanism for getting things done, it is vital that these do not splinter into hundreds of small unrelated outputs. The book therefore acts as a focal point and counter force to those centrifugal tendencies, which has been aided by the creation of 'thinking' meetings (see Section 1) and shared vision documents such as the Roadmap This process of plaiting together the thematic strands will, we hope, act to drive credit back to everyone involved in the project. We therefore expect the author list to look unlike any seen in the discipline of history heretofore.

4.4 Conclusions

In ending with the topic of authorship we might reflect on the gap between the public face of collaboration – shown via its published outputs – and the labour that goes into making those possible. It is easy to regard self-reflection on the nature of your own collaboration as a luxury or indulgence: that is, something additional to the 'real' task of a multidisciplinary research project, narrowly conceived as 'doing research'. However we take an alternative view. There is no off-the-peg template that explains how digital humanities teams operate and the specifics of our collaborative practices will not map exactly to that of any other team. However, it is our experience that teams do need to think about this problem and that this work is not something separate from the creation of outputs; it is – in the same way as obtaining data and building infrastructure – fundamental to the research process.

It is rare that we get to see behind the scenes of a project. Radical collaboration is hard, but the rewards are great, and we wish to place emphasis on the practical ways in which multidisciplinary research can be made to work. At the heart of our approach has been a process of review and iteration. From our initial Delivery Plan, through quarterly team review workshops, and our collaboratively produced Roadmaps, we have constantly sought to lay in front of our team exactly what work is being done, by whom, and to what effect. Through collective reflection, we have been able to adapt and change gears when necessary – whether in order to follow new opportunities, or to respond to unanticipated setbacks. In all cases, open communication has been the bedrock of our team's culture.

Conclusion

The breadth and nature of collaborative historical research have changed dramatically in the age of big data. As the preceding sections show, when *digital* records are the object of inquiry, new forms of collaboration are required. Digital research requires negotiation with larger institutional bodies and commercial entities often simply to ensure access to the data that is needed. It requires the negotiation of contracts and legal frameworks to ensure that access is legal. It requires the alignment of host organisations and their best practices around data storage and security. Thus significant domain-crossing is required even before the research process can begin. Furthermore, the combination of skills required for operationalising historical questions as computational queries requires a more diverse cast of actors than have hitherto turned their attention to the study of the past. The recommendations of this Element, therefore, have crossed similarly broad terrain.

Building the right team is foundational to the success of such an endeavour. This is not simply about starting with the right combination of investigators, or hiring the right expertise onto the team. It is about making time and space to develop what Peter Galison helpfully describes as 'contact languages' at the 'trading zones' between disciplines. It takes time to develop fluency when crossing such language barriers, and we urge readers beginning collaborations to provide concrete structures and spaces in their work plans for such conversations. We also recommend writing shared values (perhaps in a Project Charter) and shared objectives (e.g. in a Delivery Plans or Roadmap) in 'living documents' that are open to all members, and which are regularly edited together as a team. Indeed, we would contend that effective communication – of which documentation is a linchpin – is the ultimate key to good collaboration.

While it is vital to put in place the right foundations, collaboration must be practised in action. We recommend getting started through initial proof-of-concept work, such as our proposal of the Minimum Research Outcome (MRO). The point of the MRO is to learn enough about whether an idea works to decide whether to build on it, change it, or leave it behind. Such an approach to work, however, requires a routine of reflection and review. A regular full-team review will ensure people keep moving in the same direction, and it enables a project to decide when it needs to pivot – whether that is because the intellectual questions dictate a change in direction, or in response to unforeseen circumstances. A crucial final part of collaboration in action is ensuring that credit flows properly to all parts of a team when outputs are published or released. While goodwill goes a long way, clarity regarding who should be credited is best aided through an authorship and credit policy, which fully reflects the breadth of labour and engagement of all the constituent parts of the project. In sum, collaboration does not just 'happen': it requires active work, investment, and nourishment throughout the process of a project.

Regarding the *digital* parts of the digital history projects – the data and the infrastructure – our recommendations are offered to two separate audiences. The first are for collaborative teams and institutes concerning what they can plan for in the current research landscape (tailored especially to the UK context). We suggest that institutes and projects seeking to work on cultural heritage data should be prepared to tackle the current mixed-rights data landscape. The lack of programmatic national funding for digitisation means that a lot of the data available has been produced in partnership with commercial entities. Cultural heritage institutions have done amazing work, in the circumstances, negotiating terms that are mutually beneficial for the partners involved (compared, for instance, to the frankly exploitative open access routes offered by some for-profit academic journals). But these arrangements almost always necessitate additional labour to acquire access to the data and, once obtained, it may come with a raft of restrictions regarding how it can be used, and it places key barriers to open and reproducible research. Projects can save a lot of time by choosing to work with data that is already open access, but this entails working questions around that material rather than beginning with the research questions and finding the right data. We have also sought to demythologise the process of accessing some particular (but important) data sets, and we recommend especially phasing of work and hiring a rights manager where budget allows – although the current timeframes that data acquisition processes can entail make it incompatible with the timeframes of publicly funded projects.

Pragmatic decisions about *which data* can also help the choices you make when addressing the infrastructural choices around where you host it, and how this meets your project's requirements in terms of budget, accessibility and security. How restrictive those expectations are around security can have a major impact on workflows, human resourcing and time allocated to working with the data and finding or developing the right software and tools. More importantly, it determines how open and reproducible you can make your research in terms of publications. The expectations around establishing safe havens and other security measures, can create unnecessary burden on teams, and it is here again we encounter structural issues that really require solutions at the national scale.

This brings us to the second audience for our recommendations, funders and policymakers. Exciting opportunities are posed for research at the interface between historical inquiry, cultural heritage data, and the power of data science. For those reasons, humanities scholars are actively being urged towards such work in the UK by targeted funding calls, and by white papers from The Department for Digital, Culture, Media and Sport. But if this work is genuinely to be encouraged, it needs to be feasible for more people. Researchers who have worked and struggled with the realities need to communicate back to these corridors of power that there remain some substantial hurdles that are hampering research in this area. The cost even of *storing* large cultural heritage data sets makes ambitious digital research almost impossible within the funding ceiling of traditional project budgets. Therefore, either those budgets need to increase substantially, or a suitable centralised data and research infrastructure need to be offered to the community. However it will take time to put this in place, as the requirements are now well rehearsed in the preceding pages: the challenges of ensuring legal access to commercial data, housing it in a suitably secure environment, and making it usable to all, with the tools they need – that is, not just using built-in analytics, but allowing ways of securely manipulating the data using bespoke methods and software developed by projects to answer tailored research questions. But hopefully the more that we have these discussions, and thanks to increased investment in this area, we can move towards solutions in the coming years.

References

Ahnert R. et al. (2021). *Living with Machines Delivery Plan Version 1, 2019*. London: The Alan Turing Institute. https://doi.org/10.23636/5619-jd50.

Ahnert, R., Hetherington, J., and Tolfo, G. (forthcoming). 'The Minimum Research Outcome'. In U. Pawlicka-Deger and C. Thomson (eds.), *Digital Humanities and Laboratories: Perspectives on Knowledge, Infrastructure and Culture*, Routledge.

Arenas, D. et al. (2019). 'Design Choices for Productive, Secure, Data-Intensive Research at Scale in the Cloud'. https://arxiv.org/pdf/1908.08737.pdf.

Beals, M. H., and Bell, E. (2020). *The Atlas of Digitised Newspapers and Metadata: Reports from Oceanic Exchanges*, Loughborough. https://10.6084/m9.figshare.11560059.

Beelen, K. et al. (2022). 'Bias and Representativeness in Digitized Newspaper Collections: Introducing the Environmental Scan'. *Digital Scholarship in the Humanities,* 1–22. https://doi.org/10.1093/llc/fqac037.

Belsky, S. (2018). *The Messy Middle; Finding Your Way Through the Hardest and Most Crucial Part of Any Bold Venture*, London: Portfolio Penguin.

Bender E. (2021). 'On the Dangers of Stochastic Parrots: Can Language Models Be Too Big?' In *Proceedings of the 2021 ACM Conference on Fairness, Accountability, and Transparency* (FAccT '21). Association for Computing Machinery, New York, USA, 610–23. https://doi.org/10.1145/3442188.3445922.

Clement T. E. (2011). 'Collaborators' Bill of Rights'. In T. E. Clement and D. Reside (eds.), *Off the Tracks: Laying New Lines for Digital Humanities Scholars*, Maryland Institute for Technology in the Humanities, 9–10. https://hcommons.org/deposits/item/hc:12069/.

Cockburn, A., and Williams, L. (2001). 'The Costs and Benefits of Pair Programming'. In G. Succi and M. Marchesi (eds.), *Extreme Programming Examined*, Addison-Wesley, 223–47, London.

Coll Ardanuy, M. et al. (2020). 'Living Machines: A Study of Atypical Animacy'. *Proceedings of the 28th International Conference on Computational Linguistics,* 4534–4545. https://10.18653/v1/2020.coling-main.400.

Coll Ardanuy, M. et al. (2021). 'Station to Station: Linking and Enriching Historical British Railway Data'. *Proceedings of the Workshop on Computational Humanities Research*, Vol 2989, pp. 249–69. CHR 2021.

Adam Crymble and Julia Flanders, 'Fair Cite' Issues in Digital Humanities, 7/2 (2013)

Department for Digital, Culture, Media & Sport, (March 2016). *Culture White Paper*. London: Department for Digital, Culture, Media & Sport. www.gov .uk/government/publications/culture-white-paper.. . .

Dzogang, F. et a*l*. (2016). 'Discovering Periodic Patterns in Historical News'. *PLOS ONE*, 11, 11. https://doi.org/10.1371/journal.pone.0165736.

Filgueira, R. et al. (2019). 'Defoe: A Spark-Based Toolbox for Analysing Digital Historical Textual Data', *2019 15th International Conference on eScience (eScience)*, Vol 15, 235–42, https://10.1109/eScience.2019.00033.

Galison, P. (1997). *Image and Logic: A Material Culture of Microphysics*, University of Chicago Press.

GitLab, *The Remote Manifesto,* https://about.gitlab.com/blog/2015/04/08/the-remote-manifesto/ and https://about.gitlab.com/company/culture/all-remote/ guide/.

Gliserman, S. (1969). 'Mitchell's "Newspaper Press Directory": 1846-1907'. In *Victorian Periodicals Newsletter*, no. 4/2, 10–29.

Gooding, P., and Terras, M. (2020). *Electronic Legal Deposit: Shaping the Library Collections of the Future*, London: Facet.

Hobson, T., and Tolfo, G. (2019). 'Living with Machines – Metadata Model', https://doi.org/10.23636/1159.

Hosseini, K. et al. (2020). 'DeezyMatch: A Flexible Deep Learning Approach to Fuzzy String Matching'. *The 2020 Conference on Empirical Methods in Natural Language Processing,* 62–69.

Hosseini, K. et al. (2021). 'Maps of a Nation? The Digitized Ordnance Survey for New Historical Research'. *Journal of Victorian Culture*, 26, 284–99. https://doi.org/10.1093/jvcult/vcab009.

Intellectual Property Office (2022). 'Artificial Intelligence and Intellectual Property: Copyright and Patents: Government Response to Consultation', www.gov.uk/government/consultations/artificial-intelligence-and-ip-copy right-and-patents/outcome/artificial-intelligence-and-intellectual-property-copyright-and-patents-government-response-to-consultation.

Kemman, M. (2021). *Trading Zones of Digital History.* Berlin, Boston: De Gruyter Oldenbourg. https://doi.org/10.1515/9783110682106.

King, G. and Hopkins, J. D. (2010). 'A Method of Automated Nonparametric Content Analysis for Social Science'. *American Journal of Political Science*, 54, no. 1, 230. https://doi.org/10.1111/j.1540-5907.2009.00428.x.

Lansdall-Welfare, T. et al. (2017). 'Content Analysis of 150 Years of British Periodicals'. *PNAS*, 114, 4. https://doi.org/10.1073/pnas.1606380114

Melgar-Estrada, L. et al. (2019). 'The CLARIAH Media Suite: A Hybrid Approach to System Design in the Humanities'. *CHIIR '19: Proceedings of the 2019 Conference on Human Information Interaction and Retrieval*, 373–7. https://doi.org/10.1145/3295750.3298918.

Mendoza, N. (2017). '"The Mendoza Review": An Independent Review of Museums in England', www.gov.uk/government/publications/the-mendoza-review-an-independent-review-of-museums-in-england.

Nanni, F., 'Highlighting Authors' Contributions and Interdisciplinary Collaborations in Living with Machines', https://livingwithmachines.ac.uk/highlighting-authors-contributions-and-interdisciplinary-collaborations-in-living-with-machines/, London.

Perkel, J. M. (2018). 'Why Jupyter is Data Scientists' Computational Notebook of Choice?' *Nature*, 563, 145–6. www.nature.com/articles/d41586-018-07196-1.

Posner, M. (2022). 'Agile and the Long Crisis of Software'. *Logic*, no. 16. https://logicmag.io/clouds/agile-and-the-long-crisis-of-software/.

Rawson, R., and Muñoz, T. (2019). 'Against Cleaning'. In M. K. Gold and L. F. Klein, (eds.), *Debates in the Digital* Humanities *2019*, Minneapolis: Minnesota University Press. https://dhdebates.gc.cuny.edu/projects/debates-in-the-digital-humanities-2019.

Reiter, N. et al. (September 2017). 'To GUI or not to GUI?' In M. Eibl and M. Gaedke (eds.), *INFORMATIK 2017, Lecture Notes in Informatics (LNI)*, vol. 275, Chemnitz, Germany, 1179–84.

Rhinow, H. et al. (2012). 'Design Prototypes as Boundary Objects in Innovation Processes'. In Rhinow, H., Koeppen, E., and Meinel, C. (eds.), *Proceedings of the 2012 International Conference on Design Research Society (DRS 2012)*, Bangkok, Thailand: DRS, 1–10.

Ries, E. (3 August 2009). 'Minimum Viable Product: A Guide'. *Startup Lessons Learned*, www.startuplessonslearned.com/2009/08/minimum-viable-product-guide.html.

Rodger, R. (2020). 'Making the Census Count: Revealing Edinburgh 1760–1900'. *Journal of Scottish Historical Studies*,40, 134–48.

Ruecker, S., and Radzikowska, M. (2008). 'The Iterative Design of a Project Charter for Interdisciplinary Research'. 288–94. https://dl.acm.org/doi/10.1145/1394445.1394476.

Scholars' Lab charter, https://scholarslab.lib.virginia.edu/charter/.

Schurer, K. and Higgs, E. (2020). 'Integrated Census Microdata (I-CeM) Names and Addresses, 1851-1911: Special Licence Access' [data collection], 2nd ed., UK Data Service, SN: 7856. http://doi.org/10.5255/UKDA-SN-7856-2.

Star, S. L. (1999). 'The Ethnography of Infrastructure'. *American Behavioral Scientist*, 43, no. 3, 377–91. https://doi.org/10.1177/00027649921955326.

Terras, M. et al. (June 2018). 'Enabling Complex Analysis of Large-Scale Digital Collections: Humanities Research, High-Performance Computing, and Transforming Access to British Library Digital Collections'. *Digital Scholarship in the Humanities*, 33, no. 2, 1, 456–66. https://doi.org/10.1093/llc/fqx020.

The Turing Way Community, et al. (25 March 2019). *The Turing Way: A Handbook for Reproducible Data Science* (Version v0.0.4). Zenodo. http://doi.org/10.5281/zenodo.3233986.

Thesing, T., Feldmann, C., and Burchardt, M. (2021). 'Agile versus Waterfall Project Management: Decision Model for Selecting the Appropriate Approach to a Project.' *Procedia Computer Science*, 181, 746–56, https://doi.org/10.1016/j.procs.2021.01.227.

Wershler, D. et al. (2022). *The Lab Book: Situated Practices in Media Studies*, University of Minnesota Press. https://manifold.umn.edu/projects/the-lab-book.

'Manifesto for Agile Software Development', https://agilemanifesto.org/.

Zhang, S. et al. (2022). 'OPT: Open Pre-trained Transformer Language Models', https://doi.org/10.48550/arXiv.2205.01068.

Cambridge Elements ⹁

Historical Theory and Practice

Daniel Woolf
Queen's University, Ontario

Daniel Woolf is Professor of History at Queen's University, where he served for ten years as Principal and Vice-Chancellor, and has held academic appointments at a number of Canadian universities. He is the author or editor of several books and articles on the history of historical thought and writing, and on early modern British intellectual history, including most recently *A Concise History of History* (CUP 2019). He is a Fellow of the Royal Historical Society, the Royal Society of Canada, and the Society of Antiquaries of London. He is married with 3 adult children.

About the Series
Cambridge Elements in Historical Theory and Practice is a series intended for a wide range of students, scholars, and others whose interests involve engagement with the past. Topics include the theoretical, ethical, and philosophical issues involved in doing history, the interconnections between history and other disciplines and questions of method, and the application of historical knowledge to contemporary global and social issues such as climate change, reconciliation and justice, heritage, and identity politics

Cambridge Elements ≡

Historical Theory and Practice